STEPS AND STAGES: FROM 1 TO 3

The Toddler Years

The Toddler Years

Holly Bennett and Teresa Pittman

KEY PORTER BOOKS

Canadian Cataloguing in Publication Data

Pitman, Teresa
  Steps and Stages 1 to 3 : the toddler years

(Steps & Stages guides)
ISBN 1-55013-937-1

1. Toddlers. 2. Child development. 3. Child rearing. I. Bennett, Holly, 1957- . II. Title. III. Title: Steps and stages one to three. IV. Series: Pitman, Teresa. Steps & stages guides.

HQ774.5.P57 1998   649'.122   C97-932791-1

The publisher gratefully acknowledges the assistance of the Canada Council and the Ontario Arts Council.

Key Porter Books
70 The Esplanade
Toronto, Ontario
Canada M5E 1R4

THE CANADA COUNCIL | LE CONSEIL DES ARTS
FOR THE ARTS | DU CANADA
SINCE 1957 | DEPUIS 1957

Printed and bound in Canada

98 99 00 01 5 4 3 2 1

Contents

Acknowledgements

THERE ARE ALWAYS SO MANY PEOPLE TO THANK, but, like a good speech, we think acknowledgements should be brief.

First and foremost, our thanks to the many parents and professionals who have shared their time, their thoughts and their experiences with children so generously and so often.

Second, to our own kids, who taught us most of what we know about parenting, forgave our gazillion mistakes and continue to make our lives interesting and fun.

Finally, we send our heartfelt thanks to Fran Fearnley, former editor-in-chief of Today's Parent Group, who took a chance on both of us over ten years ago, and has been a wonderful editor, mentor and friend ever since.

First Words

WITH YOUR BABY'S FIRST BIRTHDAY (or thereabouts), you enter a whole new world. It's a good moment to take a deep breath and see how far you've come. You and your baby have weathered sleepless nights and crying jags, nursing marathons, and the worry of that first illness. Now you see the wonderful results of all that loving care: your sturdy, energetic, expressive little toddler. She can get around by herself (though not quite everywhere she wants to go); communicate her wants, needs, delights and sorrows (most of the time); and is unmistakably an individual.

Having seen your child through the intense needs of infancy, you might think you'd get a bit of a rest now. Don't get too comfortable! Even the parents who just love the toddler stage (and there are lots of us) admit that it's pretty hard work. Your toddler has many challenges to face in the next couple of years: from mastering the intricacies of language to making her first forays into independence from you. Through it all, she will be driven to explore, climb, touch, taste and test as she tries to soak up all there is to learn about the world by "toddler osmosis." It all adds up to an intense and sometimes stormy passage.

But don't be discouraged. Toddlers are also the most charming, affectionate, awe-inspiring and enjoyable people on earth. For every time you despair of getting him to do the simplest thing, there will be times when you marvel at what delightful company he is becoming. For every time you feel impatient at his clinginess or timidity, there will be times when his courageous determination to learn and grow takes your breath away. And we guarantee that even after he moves on into the relative stability of the preschool and school years, there will always be a special place in your heart for the funny little baby/child he once was.

Holly Bennett

Teresa Pitman

Torn in Two Directions:
Dependence and Independence

IF THERE'S A THEME that epitomizes toddlerhood, it's the push-me-pull-you struggle between the toddler's need for security, comforting, and plain old everyday help in her dauntless quest for the power and competence of the grown-ups around her. Not until her teens will you see such a maelstrom of back-and-forth development and changing moods and needs.

Look at the growth that goes on in this period. On her first birthday, walking is either a recent achievement, or a triumph still to come. By her third birthday, she will be running and jumping; conversing fluently; toilet-trained or close to it. She will feed herself, dress herself (mostly), ride a trike and operate the VCR better than you do. She will, in short, have made a huge leap towards independence.

Your child's own "developmental wiring" pushes her relentlessly to make that leap. It's a learning curve that would send adults into stress counselling—and it is, in fact, often stressful for kids as well. What buffers her from that stress? A retreat into babyhood, and you! A cuddle in the rocking chair, a bottle with her blanky, a carry up the stairs to preschool—these are the "battery rechargers" that reassure her that she doesn't have to grow up all at once, and that she doesn't have to give up your love when she gives up her helplessness.

Like the metamorphosis of a caterpillar to a butterfly, your toddler's transformation into a "big kid" looks pretty mixed-up at times. But trust in the process. In her own way, in her own time, she's growing her wings.

LIFE IS A ROLLER COASTER:
TODDLER GROWING PAINS

WOULD YOU PUT THAT BACK, please, Michelle?" Twelve-month-old Michelle happily toddled back to the table, carefully replacing the cut-glass vase in response to her mom's pleasant request. I was so impressed. It would be some years before I had children of my own, and I hadn't had much exposure to children's developmental cycles. Michelle was as sunny and co-operative a little girl as one could imagine, and I credited her skilful parents.

But within six months stormy weather had set in. Michelle's big blue eyes still reminded me of Tweety Bird, but *this* Tweety Bird screamed with rage when her milk spilled, fought a simple diaper change like a tiger, and wasn't the least interested in "putting that back, please." Now, when asked to relinquish some forbidden treasure she was more likely to clutch it fiercely to her chest, meet her parents' firm eye contact with her own pint-sized glare and flatly refuse. Somehow, Michelle's household didn't seem quite so calm and harmonious any more.

What went wrong?

Not a thing, reassures Vancouver parent educator Kathy Lynn. Michelle was doing exactly what her "developmental blueprint" called for her to do at this age: discovering and asserting her own independence.

"What we call 'classic twos' behaviour actually starts at anywhere from 16 to 20 months," says Lynn. "This marks the child's first major transition from infancy towards independence."

But why is it such a turbulent passage? "Remember how you felt when you were first pregnant, or starting a new, challenging job?" says Lynn. "Like you, children entering this transition are, on one hand, really excited, and at the same time, absolutely terrified. Unlike adults, though, they are experiencing this confusing set of emotions with a very

IT'S NORMAL IF . . .
- **Your toddler solemnly repeats your rule, and then immediately breaks it (because she needs to assert her will, has poor impulse control and wants to know if you really mean it).**
- **Your toddler weeps or rages over what seems, from an adult perspective, a ridiculous issue (like he wanted to turn on the light, but didn't tell you, so you did it).**
- **Your toddler gets all excited about her friend who is coming to visit, and then makes the visit a trial by clutching every toy to her chest.**

You may also see some astonishingly mature behaviours, depending on which way the wind blows that day. Which is why toddlers are the most charming and frustrating people on earth.

immature little nervous system and no previous experience to help them understand how to move through a major life change."

When parents understand that so-called toddler negativity is a normal developmental stage, not a sign of inadequate discipline, it's easier to take it in stride. "Parents can get into terrible difficulty when they take this personally," observes Lynn. "All that negativity is directed to your child's confusion and fear, not to you. You don't have to fight it. Just accept it, and trust in the ability of your child to get through it."

Okay, so we won't panic. Can we help? Definitely, says Lynn. "Parents help by easing the transition, celebrating the transition, and supporting the transition."

Easing the transition. "We do this by making success possible," says Lynn. "Life is full of failure when you're 18 months old, and it's really important for them to succeed right now." Now is the time to move from a "baby-proof" home to a "child-friendly" home: small glasses, plastic dishes, low shelves and clothing hooks, step-stools, Velcro shoes, elasticized pants—the things that allow your child to accomplish what he sets out to do. And because what he most wants to do is what big people do, creatively designing "real but tiny jobs" ("These groceries are heavy for me. Can you help by carrying this potato?") will help him feel he really is growing up.

Celebrate the transition. Of course, you have mixed feelings about his growing up, too. Some days, you wish he could stay a baby forever. But, suggests Lynn, your child doesn't need to know that. He

"Jeremy was crying so hard about his broken cookie that I actually tried to tape it together. Part of me couldn't believe what I was doing. Later I saw another mother in the same situation. She just quickly said, 'Oh, good! Now you have two cookies!' and her little girl was pleased as punch."

needs to know you're delighted with him now, in all his mixed-up toddler glory—and that you're as happy about his new achievements as he is. "Kids want to grow up, and they want to please us," says Lynn. "They shouldn't feel torn between those two desires."

Support the transition. Children's development is often an uneven, back-and-forth business—but toddlers and teenagers take the cake! Our support, says Lynn, lies in "accepting who they are in the moment—infants one second, preschoolers the next, toddlers again the next. We act like the battery recharger, allowing them to regress and plug in with us, until they're ready to take the another step forward."

Toddlers also need our support when they lose control. Frustration can't always be avoided: she may *not* bang her spoon against the window (!), and refuses any alternative; the cookie breaks in two, and no parental magic will mend it. She dissolves into wails of outrage. Maybe you feel pretty frustrated yourself! Now what? First, suggests Lynn, "remember that young kids' emotions are truly transitory, and they can go from total frustration to sunshine in an astonishingly short time. So don't make too big a deal out of it. Hold firm to your rule, if that's what it's about, but watch for the moment when your child is open to comforting—and then hold and comfort her. And when it's over, just let it go. She can't talk about it. All she needs to know is that she got through it, you were there for her, and she *still* can't bang the spoon against the window.

"This stage is a real roller-coaster ride for the child," adds Lynn. "But we don't have to ride it too. The parent helps by being a comforting seat belt, not another screaming passenger."

"I DO IT": THE QUEST FOR INDEPENDENCE

TODDLER'S REACH SO OFTEN exceeds his grasp. He has big-kid ambitions, trapped in a baby body. He senses what is possible, observes what big people do, feels his own understanding and competence blooming. But he doesn't have the judgement to choose achievable goals. And so for every new accomplishment he can glory in (and there are lots at this stage), there are, inevitably, many frustrations.

A *little* frustration can motivate a toddler and spur her on to new efforts. But when her capacity to tolerate failure runs dry, she will quickly dissolve into fury, tears, or helplessness. At times, especially if she's overtired, the least setback will overwhelm her.

Consider Ruth, 22 months, who is struggling fruitlessly—and stubbornly—with the zipper of her coat. "C'mon, Ruthie, I'll help," says her dad. "It's time to go."

"*No! I do it!*" Ruth wrenches away from Daddy's all-too-competent hands. She fiddles again with the wretched zipper, searching to replicate the effortless magic of adults.

"This is the story of her life these days," her father says with a sigh. "She has to do everything herself—even things she can't possibly manage."

Tonight, the story ends in tears. Eventually Ruth's dad has to take over, despite her frantic protest. She's somewhat mollified, though, by being invited to pull the zipper up once it's started, and as they leave the house ("Daddy carry") Ruth has regained her composure. Until next time.

Can we help smooth this tumultuous passage towards independence? Janet Libbey, daycare co-ordinator with Canadian Mothercraft, offers these suggestions.

Create success. "Try to interest them in new activities and tasks that they *can* master," suggests Libbey. Can your one-year-old carry a small

HELPING...WITH TACT

When a toddler bites off more than he can chew, it's sometimes possible to step in without completely deflating his efforts:

- "Are you stuck in your shirt? How about if I just get it over your ears—now, you pull. Look, you did it!"
- "Here's a butter knife that's safe for you. I'll just put this sharp knife away, and then you can show me how you cut up Play-Doh."
- "Only big people can pick up the guinea pig. But he would love it if you'd feed him a carrot! Can you get one out of the fridge?"
- "I'd better pour the drink. You be the boss and tell me when to stop."

bag of groceries, put potatoes in the pot, find the socks in the laundry pile? Every small success helps her feel confident in her ability to learn.

Applaud both success and effort. Of course you'll say "Good for you!" when he masters some new skill. But Libbey reminds us that kids need reinforcement for trying and failing, too: "You tried really hard to get those shoes on. That's good work!" The courage to keep trying is worth preserving.

Continue to babyproof. Some parents, seeing their child's great gains in language, feel she should now be able to understand and follow "don't touch" rules. But Libbey urges us to make our home environment toddler-friendly—not just for safety, but to minimize frustration. "Put away forbidden objects, and keep their own things easily accessible. 'No' is a word one- and two-year-olds cannot comprehend."

When possible, let them try. "They need to be allowed to practise those skills," says Libbey. "In the opening example, Ruthie's parents might start laying out her clothes well before they need to leave in the morning, so she can try dressing while they get ready for work. Or they could play 'dress-up' with coats and zippers on the weekend."

Help tactfully. But what if he's just driving himself crazy? Toddlers have been known to persist with an impossible task until they are over-

8

come with screams of rage. Better, if possible, to step in when you observe your toddler's rising frustration level—but try offering just enough help to allow *him* to succeed.

Unfortunately, our well-meaning attempts to help often just seem to add insult to injury. A two-year-old may resist your help out of wounded pride, while a one-year-old may simply misunderstand, believing you intend to take away his prize rather than open it for him. Libbey suggests, "You have to gently work your way in. Making a game of it, or adding a song, can help." At this stage, diplomacy becomes an important parental art!

"The ironic thing for a parent is, once they get big enough that they actually can do all these things, they don't want to any more. My one-year-old cries because she can't reach the coat hook, and my four-year-old cries because I won't hang up his jacket for him!"

Redirect. Sometimes you *have* to call a halt. Your older child's waiting at kindergarten, and there's no time for fiddling with sandals. Or no matter how clever it was to drag her chair over to the microwave table, she's still not allowed to use it. "Give her something else to do, to distract her," suggests Libbey. "A book, a favourite toy—something to redirect her attention—may help." Or it may not. If she still dissolves into a tantrum, "Don't make a big deal of it. Just grin and bear it, get through it, and then move on."

Finally, Libbey reminds us that toddlers don't *always* feel independent. Growing up is a daunting challenge—so it's no wonder that Mr. Do-It-Myself still wants to be carried to bed or for you to feed him sometimes. This "retreat to babyhood" helps him recharge his energy and reassures him that he doesn't have to become a "big boy" all at once. "Let them be babies when they need to," says Libbey. "Give them lots of cuddles and hugs and comforting. Reassure them that even after a stormy encounter, you still love each other."

"NO! NO! NO!": THE TODDLER'S MAGIC WORD

REAKFAST IS READY!" There were seven adults and two active toddlers gathered around the table on this holiday weekend, and the toddlers were determined to assert themselves. Two-year-old Cynthia's behaviour was classic. As her mother lifted her up to the high chair she said "*No!*" and pushed away with her feet. She wanted to sit in a regular chair. But once seated, Cynthia realized she couldn't reach the food set in front of her and started to cry. Her mother patiently pointed out the benefits of the high chair, but Cynthia wasn't giving in: "*No, no, no!*"

There were more tears, more suggestions, and a bowl of cereal growing soggier by the minute. Finally, Cynthia agreed to sit on another adult's lap while she ate her breakfast. But as we left for a morning walk, another crisis unfolded: Cynthia wanted to push her stroller, not ride in it. It was a struggle for her to keep up, and she was soon too tired to walk further. But every attempt to entice her into the stroller was met with the same response: "*No!*" Her mother eventually picked her up and set her down in the stroller despite her protests; within a minute or two Cynthia was asleep.

Neil, only a few days older than Cynthia, had his own approach. He specialized in the Silent No. His mother suggested putting on his coat to go outside, and Neil simply kept his arms folded. No arguments, no throwing toys—but he wasn't going to do it. His mother persisted, offering one option after another, and finally succeeded by suggesting he bring along the toy he was playing with.

Cynthia and Neil may have different approaches to resisting the things they don't want to do, but they're both tackling an important stage of development. They are working on becoming more independent.

This stage can be especially hard on parents because one- and two-

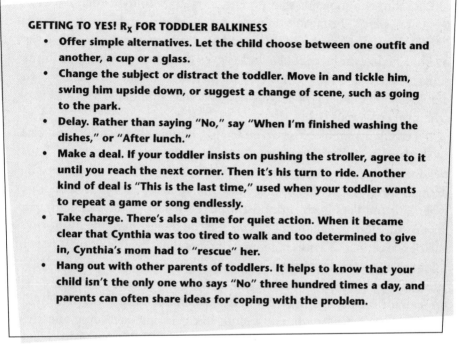

GETTING TO YES! R$_x$ FOR TODDLER BALKINESS
- **Offer simple alternatives. Let the child choose between one outfit and another, a cup or a glass.**
- **Change the subject or distract the toddler. Move in and tickle him, swing him upside down, or suggest a change of scene, such as going to the park.**
- **Delay. Rather than saying "No," say "When I'm finished washing the dishes," or "After lunch."**
- **Make a deal. If your toddler insists on pushing the stroller, agree to it until you reach the next corner. Then it's his turn to ride. Another kind of deal is "This is the last time," used when your toddler wants to repeat a game or song endlessly.**
- **Take charge. There's also a time for quiet action. When it became clear that Cynthia was too tired to walk and too determined to give in, Cynthia's mom had to "rescue" her.**
- **Hang out with other parents of toddlers. It helps to know that your child isn't the only one who says "No" three hundred times a day, and parents can often share ideas for coping with the problem.**

year-olds have limited vocabularies and often find it hard to express what it is they feel so strongly about. Neil didn't have the words to explain that he hadn't finished playing with his toy, so all he could do was refuse. And sometimes toddlers don't even know what they're protesting—but if you want them to do it, they're not going to.

Ruth Lockshin, mother of four and former toddler consultant for La Leche League Canada (an organization supporting breastfeeding), believes that it helps to understand why your child is being so negative.

"The negativism of toddlers is as legendary as adolescent rebellion, because both are times of establishing independence," she explains. "I think they're also times when parents get really negative, though, and that makes it worse."

Lockshin recommends that parents say "No" to their toddlers as little as possible, "because you're going to hear it right back." Saying "No" also makes the child feel small at a time when she is trying very hard to be big. In fact, Lockshin believes that there are very few situations when that "No" is necessary. Instead, parents can ask for the desired behaviour in a positive way: "We have to hold hands and walk when we cross the street."

Beverly Watson, director of the Early Childhood Education Centre at the University of Waterloo (Ontario), notes that many parents list "independence" as one of the most important qualities they'd like their children to develop. "We say we want to have independent children, but when our toddlers begin demonstrating their independence, many parents resist these behaviours because they challenge parental authority," she observes. But Watson reassures parents that this is a normal part of the toddler's learning process.

So there's no need to "crack down" on your negative toddler or see his balkiness as a bad habit to "nip in the bud." Learning to be independent involves more than just skills like dressing or feeding oneself— it also involves learning to think for oneself, and this is the first giant step in that long process. In all likelihood, as your child nears age three he will have less need to practise asserting his will, as he focuses more on social skills.

LITTLE KLINGONS: SEPARATION ANXIETY RETURNS

"HE FIRST TIME MY BABY buried his face into my neck when his grandpa tried to kiss him, I was ready for it," recalls Lee Jackson. "I'd read about separation anxiety and knew that late in the first year babies often become clingy with their mothers and suspicious of other people.

"What I *didn't* expect was for this behaviour to return periodically throughout the next couple of years. It seems like every few months Chris (now two) gets an attack of the Clingies, and will start following me around, demand to be carried, and cry if I go to the store without him. This might go on for a week or more—and then he'll be his old self again, doing his own thing."

SAYING GOODBYE: WHAT HELPS?
- **Leave him in familiar surroundings, with a familiar person.**
- **Tell her in advance (but in a matter-of-fact way) what will happen ("Tonight Dad and I are going out at dinnertime, and Grandma will look after you.")**
- **Give him a concrete way of knowing when you will return ("I will be back before lunch")—and do your darnedest to be on time.**
- **Give her a "transitional object"—her favourite bear, or perhaps a memento of you.**
- **Help him get involved in something fun before saying goodbye.**
- **Avoid long-drawn-out, ambiguous goodbyes. A simple "Bye-bye. See you soon" is more reassuring.**
- **If he is chasing or clutching you, pick him up, hug him, and then place him in the babysitter's arms. Now he knows there's someone there to comfort him, and you don't have to do something hurtful like push away your child or close the door in his face.**

CAN I JUST WAIT UNTIL HE'S READY?
We do, as a culture, have a tendency to rush babies' natural development. We try to "teach" the baby to sleep through the night (rather than wait for him to mature into it), "introduce" solids (rather than respond to his interest in our food), and "get him used to" separations (rather than waiting until he feels ready to step out on his own).

There *is* another way. If your own schedule and commitments allow, you can accommodate your child's clingy periods and simply keep him with you. You will probably meet with some criticism for this—but there are many babies around the world who are rarely away from their parents in the first three years or more. As he naturally becomes more adventurous, independent, and social, he will be better equipped to handle separations.

A couple of cautions, though: Do make sure your child has contact with other people and a chance to get to know at least one or two other adults. Feeling comfortable with other adult "friends" will help her move easily into the care of a babysitter when the time comes. (And give you some peace of mind should an emergency make you temporarily unable to care for your child.) Secondly, don't wait forever to introduce short separations. If your child will eventually be going to school or daycare, she needs a chance to become confident without you first.

The toddler version of recurring separation anxiety can be more trying for parents than its first appearance. It's easy to feel impatient with a child who clings to your legs at playgroup after attending happily for months, or embarrassed by a child who acts like her beloved babysitter has suddenly turned into the bogeyman. If the toddler is verbal, we feel we should be able to reason with her: "Look, I'm just having a shower. I'll be back in five minutes!" No such luck. Two-year-olds may talk, but their gut feelings still win out over mere words.

Sharon Francis Harrison teaches child development at the University of Ottawa. She explains that the initial appearance of separation anxiety, often at around nine months of age, "is the first strong indicator

TIPS FOR STARTING DAYCARE

If you're returning to work in your child's second year, the transition to daycare needs to be handled sensitively, especially if your toddler is in a "clingy" phase.

Susan Aldred, program teacher with the 12- to 24-month group at Trent Day Care in Peterborough, Ontario, says, "Ideally, we like to ease children in very gradually, starting about a week *before* the parent has to go to work. Then you can come together for a couple of hours the first day. The second day, the parent leaves for a short while. The third day, the child stays alone for longer, and maybe stays for lunch. By Friday, the child can stay for nap time, and then go right home. Even once children are "full-time," if the parents can arrange their schedule at first so as to pick the children up early— perhaps taking a shorter lunch break, for example—that helps the kids cope.

"It *is* stressful at first for both parents and children," confirms Aldred. "It's important for children to bring whatever will help make them feel comfortable. This isn't the time to wean them off their security things! For parents, good communication with staff is really important. They shouldn't hesitate to phone and check on their child whenever they're worried. And because children so often cry just momentarily when their parents leave, it can be very helpful to parents to watch for a while behind our observation window—just to see for themselves that their child really does calm down quickly."

One approach Aldred doesn't advise, though, is for parents to "pop in for a visit" during the day. "When children see their parents, they think it's time to go home, and they can be very distressed if the parents leave again. It's just too confusing and disappointing for them."

Continuity of care is very important for a young child, and every new care arrangement requires a new adjustment. Nobody changes caregivers lightly in this sensitive period. But it can turn out that your first care arrangement, no matter how carefully chosen, is not right for your child.

"Most children adapt well, within a month or so," says Aldred. "But a few do find it more difficult—some children, for example, seem to find group care overwhelming. They may do better with a family caregiver." Of course, there can also be problems with in-home and family care. If you feel your child is having trouble settling in to daycare, do share your concerns and observations with your caregiver. The solution may be to hang in a bit longer, shorten the hours the child is in care, spend some time yourself at the daycare, or have the caregiver put more effort into helping your child feel secure. As a last resort, you may need to find a more compatible care arrangement.

Choosing with Care: The Canadian Parent's Practical Guide to Quality Child Care for Infants and Toddlers, by Brenda L. Sissons and Heather McDowall Black, Addison-Wesley, 1992, is an excellent guide to finding, selecting, and monitoring care for young children.

that the baby has formed a specific attachment to a certain, special person, usually the mother." It's a positive sign—babies are supposed to want their mothers. Once a baby develops the trust and the understanding that his mom or dad always comes back, that parent's comings and goings gradually become less distressing.

When separation anxiety resurfaces during toddlerhood, the scenario is a little different. If a child has been well cared for, she has learned that you won't abandon her or drop off the face of the earth. Now she will begin to separate from you and work to become her own individual person. But it's not necessarily a smooth process.

In *Your Baby and Child*, Penelope Leach describes toddlers as see-sawing between the strong inner urge to become independent and "the contradictory desire to stay a baby." Leach feels that a toddler who becomes more clingy than usual and seems unusually worried by new places and people may be telling us that he is feeling "a little pressured, perhaps, to grow up faster than he feels he easily can...If you pick up this kind of cue from your toddler and offer a large extra ration of affection, attention and protection for a few days or weeks, the see-saw will swing back to the level again. If you miss the cues, it may tip further into anxiety."

What about those necessary separations? When the Clingies strike we can accommodate our toddler's wish to be carried upstairs to bed or follow us to the laundry room. We might even pack her along to the hairdresser's or dentist's. But we can't bring our lives to a halt. Jobs or volunteer commitments are still there; nursery school still meets two mornings a week. Can we help our kids weather these goodbyes?

First, suggests Leach, leave her with a familiar caregiver. Save new faces for a time when she's in a more adventurous frame of mind. A "transitional object," whether her favourite bear or a souvenir of you (photo, scarf, etc.), may help to console her once you're gone.

Keep your actual goodbye short and routine, says Francis Harrison. "If you always say goodbye at daycare in the same way, that's a reassuring ritual that helps a child know what to expect. If you drag out the leave-taking when he makes a fuss, it gives him the impression that his protest is working, that you might really stay. It raises his hopes only to dash them when you finally do leave."

She notes that children who have developed a trust in their parents will usually cope well with routine separations. "They will still make that fuss," she warns. "And that's legitimate. They don't want you to go, and at this age their feelings are very strong. But once you're gone, they recover quickly." Obviously it's important for your own peace of mind to get feedback from your caregiver about how easily your child "settles in" after you leave.

But *do* say goodbye. How can he allow himself to let go of your leg if he thinks you might sneak off when his back is turned? "Part of the reason parents are tempted to do this is to avoid the tears when they leave," says Francis Harrison. "It's not a nice feeling to walk away from a crying child. But he needs to have a chance to say goodbye. If you sneak off, you break trust with your child."

17

ME AND MY BLANKY: SECURITY BLANKETS AND OTHER "LOVEYS"

YOU'RE HEADING OUT TO VISIT your sister for the weekend, trying to get out of town before rush hour. Forty-five minutes into the journey, panic strikes. As you rummage fruitlessly in the assortment of bags and boxes wedged beside you, the fretful wails from the car seat rise in pitch. He needs his blanky. You *must* have packed it. The alternatives are chilling: turn the car around and fight traffic all the way home to get the *blankety blank* thing, or face a cold-turkey weekend without it. Your relief when you finally unearth a grimy snippet of flannel with frayed satin edging is at least equal to your baby's. Peace reigns in the car.

Not all babies develop this passionate attachment to one particular blanket, bear, or clutch ball. But many do, and moments like this one—when the fact sinks in that the whole family is dependent on a rag for its peace of mind—may lead parents to wonder if they ought to discourage such attachments. Are "security blankets" of any real benefit to toddlers, or just an inconvenient habit?

In his book *Toddlers and Parents*, author and paediatrician T. Berry Brazelton argues strongly that "loveys," as he calls them, are especially important to today's children:

> In a society which fosters as much early independence as ours does, it seems obvious that we as parents must also respect the importance of balances to this expensive independence. I feel it is an important kind of learning for a child to be able to comfort herself, to subside with a familiar, beloved crutch.

Lynn Tarzwell agrees. Her five-year-old daughter, Helen, still occasionally "thinks" with the "Magic Blanky" (or "Blank," for short) that

THUMB-SUCKING AND PACIFIERS

Many parents encourage their young infants to suck on a pacifier or their own thumbs for comfort—but then become uncomfortable with the habit once the first (or second) birthday comes and goes. But many toddlers still have a strong need to suck.

If the sight of your older toddler with a soother in his mouth really bothers you—or if you feel it's interfering with his ability to play and communicate with people—you might consider gradually limiting its use. Guidelines like "only in the house, because we might lose it if we take it outside," or "only in your bed, to help you sleep or relax" are often much easier for a young child to adjust to than total banishment.

Obviously, you can't throw away your child's thumb! Don't worry; there's no need to. Dr. T. Berry Brazelton is reassuring about thumb-sucking at this age: "...when one stops to realize that it is one of the few autonomous resources a small child has at his disposal for retreating, for handling tension, for comfort, it must be obvious that the things which happen in the second year make it the peak year for the need for finger- and thumb-sucking. I am relieved when a child demonstrates this kind of resourcefulness."

Will thumb-sucking affect your child's bite? Not at this age, most dentists agree. But they do like to see the child give it up by age four or five, when the permanent teeth are preparing to erupt. Frequent thumb-sucking in the early school years *can* lead to orthodontic problems, so consult with your dentist if your older preschooler is still hooked on her thumb.

has been with her since her birth. Overall, Lynn feels, it "has made life immensely easier for us and for Helen." The Tarzwells have travelled a good deal with Helen, and found her blanket helped her adapt quickly to new beds and new situations. "It was like a little bit of home away from home," reflects Lynn. "It made any bed a familiar bed, and it helped her recharge when she was stressed or tired."

Catherine Heffernan didn't realize that her daughter, Kaitlin, had a special blanky until she tried to lend it to someone else. "My little nephew had fallen asleep at Kaitlin's first birthday party, so I covered him up with a crib quilt my friend had made for Kaitlin. She had an absolute fit...and that's been her blanky ever since."

Kaitlin, now two, uses the quilt mostly for sleeping and quiet times. Like many toddlers, she's developed a special ritual with the quilt, holding one particular corner while she sucks her thumb. Catherine feels that the blanky helps Kaitlin to settle in to new places—her babysitter's or the cottage—and helps her tolerate long car trips.

Some toddlers never become attached to a special object. Since "loveys" tend to be used to provide comfort when the parents aren't there (for example, when falling asleep in the crib), babies who are rarely separated from their parents may be less likely to feel the need for a substitute. Is there anything wrong with this? Not at all! If your baby shows no interest in loveys, the most likely reason is that she does not need one—either because of her own confident, independent nature, or because her security blanket is...you! If it's the latter situation, though, be sure that any child-care provider you leave her with is willing to offer a similar style of nurturing to yours.

What happens when a "lovey" is literally loved to death—or worse, lost? Parents of children with loveys do have an extra responsibility: trying to make sure it isn't lost, and helping them find a substitute in case it is. It's a real bereavement if that special bear gets left behind, so you can't take it lightly. When Helen Tarzwell lost her magic blanky at Disneyworld, her parents were nearly as worried as she was. "To our relief, she was so tired on that trip that she actually slept okay," recalls Lynn. "When we got back to Ottawa my mother (who had made the first one) made her another with the same material on one side."

Brazelton approves of this attempt to bridge the old and the new. He advises, "If it begins to fall apart and cannot be mended or refilled, find another, more durable toy (or blanket). Tie or sew the old 'lovey' to the new one until all the old smells, sensations, and feelings have been transferred to the new one. Then, and only then, the old one can be discarded. As you can see, I feel strongly about an eighteen-month-old baby's need for all the supports he can get."

A toddler's dependence on that special soft blanket or toy certainly has its drawbacks, especially when no substitute will do. And it's important not to overuse it—to give your child a blanket or pacifier when comforting from Mom or Dad is really what's needed. But Catherine and Lynn are convinced that security blankets are a positive thing. "It's a cue, a symbol of comfort," says Lynn. "I have a new baby now and her blanket is already made and ready to roll."

"TOO SCARY!": FEARS AND PHOBIAS

WHAT ARE TODDLERS AFRAID OF? It is rarely the things we *want* them to be cautious of: hot stoves, busy streets, and deep water, for instance. But their growing imagination and awareness can lead to dramatic fears as well as new pleasures and achievements. In fact, a toddler's fears can cause a lot of stress for both parent and child. George Koblyk, a recently retired psychology professor at Mohawk College in Hamilton, Ontario, says, "Children's fears aren't really much different from the fears and worries of adults, and they can be just as upsetting to the child—even though parents may see them as irrational or trivial."

Koblyk lists several sources of fears in toddlers:

Feelings of inferiority and helplessness: Babies live a demand-free life. Once they are walking and talking, however, adults begin to have higher expectations of them. Koblyk believes that parents often make excessive demands on their toddlers, and when the toddler can't live up to them, he feels like a failure.

The toddler's new awareness of his own limitations and vulnerability can also make him fearful. Penelope Leach points out that "really, this fear response is an intelligent reaction. A baby, in a way, is repeating the experience and history of the whole human race. In ancient times, that strange animal might have been a sabre-toothed tiger. Screaming in fear might have saved his life."

Parents may make their children supersensitive to danger by constantly warning them: "Watch out for that dog, it could bite you; don't eat that, it could be poison; don't touch that, it's sharp; come away from there, you could fall." The impression the child gets, Koblyk says, is that the world is a pretty dangerous place, and he doesn't have the resources to deal with these dangers.

Development of imagination: Some fears, Koblyk explains, are "concrete displacements of inner hostile conflicts." All that means is that the toddler is able to use his imagination to dream up a scary monster or other creature that in some way symbolizes scary feelings he is experiencing inside. Koblyk uses the example of the Incredible Hulk—an ordinary man who was transformed into a green monster when he was angry. In much the same way, children can imagine monsters under the bed that represent their angry feelings, just like in Maurice Sendak's book *Where the Wild Things Are*.

> **WHEN THE FEARFUL TODDLER NEEDS HELP** In general, your patience and support will see your toddler through his fears. But if fearfulness in general, or specific fears, are so long-lasting or intense that they affect the quality of your child's life—preventing him from playing freely or making everyday outings or activities a misery—a child therapist may be of help. Ask your child's doctor for a referral.

Inborn fear tendencies: Koblyk points out that some fears are a normal, expected part of a child's development. The fear of strangers, for example, is expected to develop between ages six and eight months, and a fear of being separated from parents normally develops around 12 months and can last until the child is five years old. As well, children have different personalities and some are simply more fearful and more likely to react to real or imagined dangers. Often, Koblyk adds, it is the bright, imaginative child who is more sensitive and reacts this way. These children will always need more reassurance and help in coping with fears.

Learned fears: Toddlers are great copycats. If a mother screams every time she sees a spider, pretty soon her son will have picked up the idea that spiders are scary things. Children can also have negative experiences that teach them to be afraid of certain things, Koblyk says. For example, the toddler may have had several doctor's visits in a row that included painful immunizations, and this will lead to a fear of going to the doctor's office.

How can parents help their children cope with fears? Koblyk stresses that these behaviours are normal. "Don't overreact and think something is wrong with your child, and don't ridicule him for being afraid. Comfort him. Take his fears seriously. If he can't express his fears, it can lead to problems such as stuttering or sleeping disorders. Let him know it's okay to be scared, and that it will get better."

"One day a black Labrador bounded into the back yard where my son and two other toddlers were playing. He didn't bark or jump on them, let alone attack, but his sudden appearance terrified all three of them. For months after, they talked about the 'big black dog' and worried about whether it would come."

Decreasing the pressure and demands on the child may help. For example, if your child is scared of the dark, give her a nightlight or flashlight—or just leave the light on.

As well, Koblyk suggests playing games or telling stories in the dark with the child to help her feel more comfortable. It also helps to give the child as much control as possible. "One little boy was afraid of the bathroom fan until his parents attached a switch that allowed him to turn it on and off."

Parents can also use fantasy to help a child overcome fears. Carol Wysocki says she taught her daughter, Koral, early on that she could scare away animals such as cats and birds by clapping her hands. Now, Koral uses the same technique for imaginary monsters and scary dreams. "Koral loves *Beauty and the Beast*, but she's also scared of the Beast and sometimes has nightmares about him. So we tell her to clap her hands and he'll go away, and then she calms right down."

When fears must be confronted, Koblyk urges parents to "allow the child to confront the fear at his own pace rather than at your pace." The toddler who is afraid of dogs might look at pictures of dogs first, then watch some dogs playing on the other side of the fence. If he wants to leave after a few seconds, that's okay. A slow, gradual approach is essential. "We often feel exasperated with, or critical of, the fearful child,"

MOST COMMON TODDLER PHOBIAS

Penelope Leach reports in *Your Baby and Child* that "more than half of all children develop at least one phobia during their second and third years." (A phobia differs from an "ordinary fear" in its intensity and scope: people with a phobia about spiders, for example, don't just fear a spider in the flesh, they become anxious looking at pictures of spiders or even thinking about them.) What are they so scared of? In Western countries, writes Leach, toddlers are most often frightened of:

- Dogs
- Darkness
- Monsters
- Insects and reptiles (especially snakes)
- Loud noises (like fire alarms and sirens)

Koblyk says, "but when they're scared is when they need us to be on their side more than ever."

Carol has found that the secret to success with Koral is "allowing her to warm up to new things and new situations at her own pace. She's cautious, but she's not very fearful." That's the kind of support that toddlers need to overcome their fears and develop confidence in themselves as they grow.

The Basics:
Sleeping, Eating, Toilet Training

Brenda Cooke

THOUGH BODILY FUNCTIONS ARE not quite so front-and-centre as they were during infancy, there are still plenty of parental concerns in this department.

Sleep continues to be a hot issue (or even a desperate craving) for many parents. Parents who took night waking in stride in the first year are sometimes shocked to find that, popular mythology notwithstanding, it can be a long time before toddlers sleep regularly through the night. Even the lucky families whose toddlers sleep well at night, are likely to face bumps in the road as nap needs and bed-time routines change.

Food concerns centre around weaning and "picky eating." Breastfeeding toddlers is still fairly unusual in North America, and mothers may feel pressured to wean even when they would be happy to continue. Meanwhile, mealtimes can be difficult as toddlers become less hungry and more opinionated about everything—including what's "yucky" and how long they're willing to sit at the table!

And then there's toilet training. Thanks, perhaps, to Sigmund Freud, potty-training sometimes causes more anxiety than it deserves. Think of it as simply a skill to learn, like dressing yourself, or learning to read, not a childhood trauma or a "discipline" problem. With a relaxed, positive attitude, and a little patience, it's quite possible to actually enjoy the transition out of diapers.

But whatever *your* attitudes to all these issues, your toddler will make it clear—if you haven't already realized it—that he is a key player in this game! A parenting approach that looks for *family* solutions that meet the needs of children and grown-ups both will serve you well in the years to come.

BEDTIME IS BEAUTIFUL: CHANGING
BEDTIME ROUTINES

YOUR NEWBORN WAS NURSED or rocked to sleep, or maybe you just laid her down when she seemed tired and she closed her eyes and drifted off. Napping and waking periods were scattered, quite unpredictably at first, through the day and night.

Now picture her bedtime at age four or five. Probably you're seeing a more mature, predictable sleep pattern. Most parents expect to tuck their preschooler into bed at about the same time each night, in about the same way, and for their child to sleep until about the same time in the morning. Probably, too, you're picturing a story, song or quiet talk together as part of the routine, rather than nursing, rocking or walking.

Those are all realistic goals, but your child won't get there overnight. If you have a toddler, chances are she is somewhere between a "baby" sleep routine and a "big kid" one. That's normal—toddlers are, after all, almost by definition in a state of transition—but it can be awkward to manage, too. One day he has two naps, and then you can't get him to bed until past *your* bedtime. Another day he barely closes his eyes, but then he falls asleep in his supper. Or he'll let his dad read him stories and rub his back at bedtime, but with you he still insists on nursing to sleep.

"At around 18 months children hit a developmental turning point," explains Lorraine Gilman, workshop co-ordinator at Information Children at Simon Fraser University in B.C. "Between one and two, children experience many changes, including, often, changes in the amount of sleep and food they need."

Although sleep patterns are changing now, or maybe *because* they are, most experts suggest that this is a good time to introduce a bedtime routine that is reasonably stable. "You don't want to be locked in and too rigid, but a bedtime routine is helpful," says Gilman. "If there are cues at a particular time of day, this helps the brain say, 'Oh, time to slow down and rest.' It helps children learn to calm themselves down towards sleep."

Given the differences in development among one- and two-year-olds, not to mention differences in temperament, in their parents' preferences, and in family logistics, it's not so surprising that toddler bedtime routines come in all shapes and sizes. Let's take a peek at how some families handle this daily ritual:

Aisha Toor's third child, Amir, just turned two. Aisha says, "I think children like a little order in their lives. We try for a 'flexible routine.' I think the most important thing is that we try to keep the bedtime routine simple and short—bath, PJs, story, bed—and we focus on getting him into bed."

Although Amir's bedtime routine looks pretty "grown-up," Aisha adds that he is still nursing, and "about 98 percent of the time, the routine has included nursing at night." As he gradually weans, the bath/story routine will still be there for Amir as a familiar constant.

At 20 months, Molly Adamson is also still nursing, but not at bedtime. Her dad, Scott, isn't completely happy with their routine, although it seems to work well for Molly. "Now that she's on a mattress on the floor, one of us usually lies down beside her and pats her on the back until she goes to sleep," says Scott. Which would be fine, except that "I'm an early sleeper, so when I lie down with Molly, I usually end up falling asleep, too, and then I'm stuck having to 'get up and go to bed.' It sort of takes away my evening..."

Although the bedtime story is traditional, some toddlers aren't interested in books when they're tired, and others settle down more easily with the lights off. Singing is a nice alternative, giving the child something interesting and pleasant to focus on while demanding less concentration than a story. Beth Ayers's third child, Daniel, "loves his bed," and has always fallen asleep by himself in his crib, so their bedtime routine is pretty straightforward. "He has a special blanket that he only gets when it's bedtime or naptime," says Beth. "He doesn't drag it around

NAP STRATEGIES

"Jamie still needs a nap, but he's not tired right after lunch. He tends to fall asleep around three, or even later, waking up grumpy and disoriented around dinnertime. Then he's "Mr. Energy" just when I'd like him to go to bed..."

The transition from two naps to one, and from one to none, tends to be hard on everyone. Mostly you just have to ride it out, but here are some strategies that can ease the pain a bit:

- Toddlers who are new to giving up their morning naps tend to fall asleep face-down in their high-chair over lunch. Then they wake up starved. Follow Winnie-the-Pooh's system ("I'm feeling a little eleven-o'clockish") and serve lunch in the late morning until she builds up her stamina. If it's the afternoon nap that's been missed, dinner at "teatime" might be in order.

- To avoid the accursed late afternoon nap (favoured by older toddlers who can't quite give it up altogether), you can: hang on grimly to an earlier naptime through car rides, long walks in the stroller, cuddles in the hammock, whatever will encourage sleep right after lunch; or if he insists on staying awake until four, try waking him up after about forty-five minutes. Some kids cope well with this; others wake up unhappy and stay that way, so it may not be worth the misery.

- Later naptimes can lead to a sort of time-lapse spiral: she naps later, so she stays up later, so she wakes up in the morning later, so she naps even later... If your schedule is flexible and you don't mind, you can just wait patiently; eventually she'll give up the nap and bedtime will self-correct. Your other option is to "reset" her clock by waking her up at the "normal" time in the morning...again, easier said than done with some kids.

- Even when their children no longer need an actual sleep during the day, some clever parents manage to institute a "quiet time" after lunch, giving themselves an hour alone on the couch while their kids look at books or listen to a tape in their rooms. Definitely worth a try.

with him. That's sort of a signal that it's time to sleep. We sit together and I sing to him—maybe two or three songs. We say his prayers. We talk about the day. All this takes a few minutes, not hours. He holds his blanket and I tuck him into bed and he goes to sleep."

Val McTaggart and her husband, Robin, have a more drawn-out bedtime with their 16-month-old daughter, Katie. "I usually nurse her to sleep, or Robin rocks her, but we have a fairly long 'quiet play' time before that. She sits on our bed and we read books and do puzzles and put blocks into containers. This is sort of a family time together, so we don't rush it." While Katie falls asleep unusually late (most nights around 11:00 p.m.), Val and Robin don't fret about it: "That's just been

---

FROM CRIB TO BED

When will your child be ready to move to a big bed? Usually, the answer is "when he figures out how to climb out of a crib." That means some kids will sleep happily in their crib until age three, while junior mountain climbers may be safer moving out in early toddlerhood.

Scott Adamson's first child, Codey, had a bad fall from his crib at ten months, so they moved him to a mattress on the floor. "The mattress seemed safer than a high bed, and we used it for our next child, Molly, too."

The features of a bed can be advantages or disadvantages, depending on your bedtime expectations. "Bedtimes are a lot nicer now that Hanna is in a bed," says her mom, "because I can cuddle in beside her. We look at books while she snuggles under her covers, and often she falls asleep while I'm reading. And if she wakes up at night now, I just go and lie down with her."

On the other hand, if parents can get in more easily, so can children get out. Toddlers who have always fallen asleep on their own in a crib may suddenly be wandering out of bed after their parents. It may take many firm trips "back to bed" before they learn to stay put.

Finally, if your child tends to wander at night rather than call for you, you'll want to use a baby gate across his doorway to keep him safe.

---

her natural rhythm since day one, and we've followed her routine as opposed to trying to fight it. This makes bedtime a nice time."

Gilman points out that some children do need more help than others in managing the transition to sleep: "This is about the ability to self-soothe. Children differ in their ability to do this. Some children need a lot of external cues (i.e., a longer bedtime routine) to help them settle down—babies who need a lot of rocking and walking before falling asleep will often need more attention as toddlers, too. And some children don't tolerate change very well. Any upset in routine sends them all out of kilter. Others are more adaptable, and for them, consistency around bedtime doesn't matter so much."

Your bedtime routine will evolve to meet the changing needs of your child and your family, but your basic goal won't change. "You want to make bedtime a wonderful part of the day, not a nightmare struggle," says Gilman. In all families, there will be times when, as Scott Adamson says ruefully, bedtime is something you "get through" rather than enjoy. But if it's like that night after night, take a look at your bedtime routine. A new approach might just get you closer to the peaceful, happy "Night-night" you and your child both want.

"I used to lie down with our toddler and sing to her at bedtime, which was nice most of the time, but sometimes went on and on. I remember spending most of New Year's Eve in our friends' spare room, trying to get Kerry to sleep and feeling more and more frustrated. Then, in a quiet moment, I heard 'Baa, Baa Black Sheep' being hummed in the room next door—our hostess was doing the same thing with her little boy! We both emerged, half asleep, just before midnight..."

THE NIGHT SHIFT: COPING WITH NIGHT WAKING . . . *STILL*

"YOU MEAN HE'S *STILL* WAKING up at night?!" You cringe at the question. It seems that yours is the only 18-month-old in the world who doesn't sleep ten hours in a row. But don't believe it. One of the best-kept secrets of parenthood is this: *lots* of toddlers wake up at night. And lots of parents are tired. But what's worse, many also feel embarrassed, or even guilty, about their midnight encounters.

Some sleep experts are quick to blame childhood sleep problems on parental mismanagement. But Dr. David Haslam (bless his heart) points to research that shows that some babies sleep for shorter periods and are more difficult to settle right from birth. You probably didn't *teach* your baby to wake up.

Now let's put the problem in context.

If your child wants a 3:00 a.m. cuddle, and your energy level is okay, odds are you're not too concerned about the situation. Beth Davis, for example, says, "It doesn't affect my sleep needs that much. It's just something that I do; it comes with having children." After all, toddlers are not very independent during the day. It's not surprising, then, that they want us when they wake at night.

Laura Clemes, on the other hand, went through a harrowing few months with her toddler, Christopher, when "he didn't just wake up, he was ready to party. I'd be up with him for at least an hour several times a night. I really need my sleep and it was driving me close to insane." At two, Christopher still wakes up frequently, but he usually settles back down quickly when he's tucked in. Now, says Laura, "it's more of an annoyance than a big deal."

Night waking becomes a major problem when it interferes with par-

TEMPERAMENT AND SLEEP

Your own parenting style and energy level have an obvious influence over your approach to night waking. Your child's temperament completes the equation. Clear, apparently inborn differences have been demonstrated in traits such as arousability, regularity, persistence, and sensitivity to stimuli. These traits affect how easily a baby falls asleep and stays asleep, and sometimes cluster into an overall temperament that's been labelled "high need."

The very traits that make high-need babies and toddlers poor sleepers—high arousability and sensitivity, poor self-regulation, etc.—also work against "training" them to sleep by letting them cry. The more they cry, the more aroused they tend to get, and the harder it is for them to relax into sleep.

Some toddlers adapt quickly and easily to sleep training programs. High-need toddlers often don't. There's a clear difference between 20 minutes of fussing, and hours of frantic screaming. Observe your child, and try to find an approach to sleep that suits her temperament as well as your needs.

ents' ability to function well. Exhausted people are not very resilient, or even pleasant to live with. But what can you do?

First of all, it's important to take care of yourselves. Share the load in whatever way works for your family. Laura found things were better when her husband took over most night duty: "He seems to need less sleep than me." In other families, Mom gets up but gets weekend sleep-ins. Kim Dolan says, "I gave myself permission to take a morning off sometimes. I figured I worked hard during the night!" Talking to other parents gives you support and maybe new strategies; odds are someone you know is sleep-deprived too.

Now for your child.

The most common advice is to "Let him cry it out." Many doctors still advocate this as the way to "retrain" a night waker. A modified version (sometimes referred to as "Ferberizing," after Dr. Richard Ferber,

SLEEP BOOKS
Sleepless Children: A Handbook for Parents, by Dr. David Haslam, Pocket Books, 1985. Out of print, but well worth tracking down (ask for an interlibrary loan if your local library doesn't carry it) for its supportive, practical approach.

The Baby Book: Everything You Need to Know About Your Baby—From Birth to Age Two, by William Sears, MD, and Martha Sears, RN, Little, Brown, 1993. For a sensitive and flexible approach to night waking that's especially useful for parents of high-need babies, see chapter 15: "Nighttime Parenting: How to Get Your Baby to Sleep."

a leading proponent) requires going in to your crying child at specified intervals, to reassure him that he's fine, that you love him dearly, but that it's time for sleeping right now. The theory goes that over a few nights the child's crying periods will get progressively shorter, as he learns that there's no "payoff" to waking up.

It's not as easy as it sounds. Laura and her husband tried it, and Christopher's sleep patterns did become a little more civilized. But, recalls Laura, "it was really hard for me. I kept wondering if maybe he really needed my attention, and here I was refusing to help him." Even if you're convinced it's for everyone's good, listening to your baby cry in the dark is emotionally harrowing for most parents. You'll need a lot of support, from your spouse, from your friends the next day, maybe from a good how-to book you can reread at 3:00 a.m.

Another deterrent to the "crying" method is that already-tired parents may not be able to face a week of even more terrible sleep. Says Helen Wills, "You just do whatever gets you back to sleep fastest, even if it's not a long-term solution." Active or older toddlers may complicate the situation further with a Houdini-like ability to climb (or fall) out of their cribs, with potentially dangerous consequences.

Other parents just don't feel right about leaving their child to cry alone. "They may stop crying," says Melisande Neal, "but it teaches them not to trust you any more."

Melisande and her husband eventually brought their wakeful two-year-old into bed with them, and became sold on the family bed. "I was just a basket case, I was so tired. But once he was in with us, instead of becoming wide awake, he'd snuggle right back to sleep. We all got so much more rest." Dr. Haslam reports in his book, *Sleepless Children*, "I received more letters quoting bed-sharing as a success story than any other solution." Some parents, though, get even less sleep when a squirmy toddler shares their bed. They may find that a small mattress on the floor of their bedroom, or having the toddler share a double bed with an older sibling, can provide the same nighttime reassurance. It all depends on your own—and your baby's—sleep styles.

Finally, you may want to consider a gradual behavioural change program. The goal is to change your child's falling-asleep behaviour one easy step at a time, until she is able to go to back to sleep by herself when she wakes up. For example, if you usually rock her to sleep, you might start with replacing the rocker with a plain chair. Towards the end of the program, you might stand in the doorway, talking softly to her. Eventually, you may be able to just call reassuringly from your bed. If this approach appeals to you, Dr. Haslam's book will help you develop a suitable plan.

If some babies never sleep through, they do all grow up. "It's already a dim memory," says Kim Dolan. "They really aren't little for long." In the meantime, she advises, "Try to focus on what happens through the day, not at night." Whether your baby's waking is a minor disturbance or a major stress factor, it's only one aspect of his total self. He's still a wonderful kid.

"I'M HUNGRY!": EATING HABITS AND FOOD CHOICES

JOANNE WOOD RECALLS THAT two-year-old Ashley was "a great eater," until she hit 18 months. As a baby and one-year-old, she'd gobbled down infant cereal and strained vegetables enthusiastically. But around the middle of her second year, Ashley's appetite started to decrease and her willingness to eat everything that was put in front of her vanished. "She did a complete turnaround," Wood says.

Ashley's a pretty typical toddler, according to Sarah Lynch-Vogelzang, RD, a nutritionist with the City of Toronto Public Health Department. After the rapid growth of the first year of life, the toddler's growth rate slows down, and appetite naturally decreases, too. Lynch-Vogelzang points out: "Parents are often surprised when they see how small the portions are for toddlers. For example, two to three tablespoons of fruit is a full serving, and four ounces of juice over the whole day is plenty for a toddler."

It isn't just that toddlers eat less than their parents expect, though. They are also developing strong opinions about what they like and don't like. As Wood says: "Ashley used to like fruit salad, but now I have to give her all the fruit separate. She doesn't want her food mixed together any more. And one week she'll love broccoli, the next week she won't touch it."

Lynch-Vogelzang says that's typical, too, and the key to managing this stage is not making a big fuss about it. She says that researchers have found toddlers actually eat more when the food is placed in front of them and then ignored, than toddlers who have parents or other adults encouraging them to eat. If a toddler dislikes a certain food, Lynch-Vogelzang advises saying: "That's okay, you don't have to eat it." Toddlers who know it's okay not to finish the entire serving of a

TODDLER SNACKS

When your toddler is hungry between meals, try to think about which food groups might be a little low today. Did he eat his burger at lunch but ignore the vegetables? Then plan a snack to fill in that gap—steamed snow peas, perhaps, or cauliflower with dip. Has he been enjoying plenty of summertime fruits but ignoring protein foods? Offer cubes of cheese with whole-grain crackers, or peanut butter spread on a tortilla and rolled up.

Try some of these other nutritious and satisfying snacks for your hungry toddler:

- Plain yogurt with fruit (peaches, pears, applesauce, banana) added
- Banana mashed together with wheat germ and orange juice
- Frozen fruit juice or frozen fruit and yogurt popsicles
- Milk and fruit, whipped together in a blender for a "milkshake"
- Sandwiches made with a little cream cheese and cucumber slices
- Dry breakfast cereal in a cup—add some fruit if you like
- Spread peanut butter on lettuce and roll it up (honestly, lots of toddlers like this!)
- Cold chicken, cut into bite-size pieces
- Shredded carrots and cabbage, mixed with a little mayo and raisins

Be creative! Toddlers often enjoy flavour combinations that seem weird to adults, so don't be afraid to give something different a try.

certain food are more likely to try new things, she finds.

"However, I would definitely offer the food again in a couple of weeks, even though he rejected it this time," she says. "Toddlers' tastes are always changing. Sometimes they have to try a food 15 or 20 times before they decide they like it."

Toddler appetites are also easily affected by other variables, according to Lynch-Vogelzang. If they're tired, overexcited, not feeling well (because they are cutting teeth or coming down with a virus) or full because they've been drinking a lot of juice or milk, they may have little interest in eating. Some busy toddlers also find it hard to sit still through an entire meal. There are too many other interesting things vying for their attention.

Wood says that when Ashley announces "All done," she doesn't try to persuade her to keep eating. Instead she transfers any leftover food to a little plastic tray (as long as it isn't too messy) and sets it down near where Ashley is playing. "Often she'll come over and nibble at her food while she plays," Wood says. "She doesn't even notice that she's having the rest of her lunch or dinner."

"All three of our kids have gone from eating just about anything, at one, to being a totally picky eater by three. And even now, with the third, it still bugs me that she rejects so many things she used to like. But at least now I know from experience that she won't starve."

Ashley likes her food cut into bite-size pieces, Wood adds, and finger foods, things she can just pick up and pop into her mouth, are always preferable. Lynch-Vogelzang also encourages serving small amounts; it's better for your toddler to ask for seconds rather than have her overwhelmed by a too-large serving of food.

What about the toddler who seems to refuse an entire food group, usually vegetables? Lynch-Vogelzang suggests preparing the foods in a different way: the toddler who hates salad may enjoy cooked vegetables or grated carrots and cabbage with a little dressing. Wood says she "doctors up the food, putting a cheese sauce or salad dressing on the vegetables, for example." You can also sometimes smuggle less-popular foods into pasta sauces and casseroles (purée them to hide the evidence). Remember, too, that most of the important nutrients in vegetables can be obtained from fruits as well.

Wood comments that when Ashley has one of those "ravenous" days when she's eating enthusiastically, she sees it as a great opportunity to load up on vegetables and other less-favoured foods.

Lynch-Vogelzang suggests establishing a rhythm to your toddler's meals. "A toddler usually will have breakfast, then a snack, lunch, a

FOOD SAFETY

Toddlers are at a dangerous age when it comes to food. Most don't have enough teeth to chew really well, and they are inclined to run, talk or laugh with food in their mouths. That means parents need to be aware of potential food hazards, and always stay close by when their toddler is eating.

According to one study, the foods that most commonly cause choking are:

- **Hot dogs**
- **Nuts**
- **Hard candies**
- **Grapes**
- **Popcorn**

Small children have also been known to choke on carrots, apple pieces, beans and bread (especially white bread spread with peanut butter, which can form a gluey ball if not chewed thoroughly). These foods should not be fed to toddlers unless they have been modified to make them less dangerous. For example, hot dogs should be cut in quarters lengthwise and then cut in small pieces, grapes should be cut in halves or quarters, carrots and apples can be grated or cooked, sandwiches can be cut in "fingers" to encourage smaller bites.

It's not a good idea to give your toddler food in the car, because if he or she does choke you might find it difficult to get the car over to the side of the road quickly enough.

snack, supper, and then another snack, and these should all be served at about the same time each day. If your child gets overly hungry, he or she won't eat as well."

The snacks should be considered part of the child's overall nutrition and be selected from the food groups. Lynch-Vogelzang also thinks treats such as candy, cookies and potato chips have a place in the toddler meal plan. "If they never get these things, they end up wanting them all the time," she says. "But serve them only occasionally, in moderate amounts, and don't use them as rewards."

While mealtimes with toddlers can be messy, parents should try to keep them relaxed and pleasant. "You know your toddler is going to spill things and make a mess," Lynch-Vogelzang says, "so plan for it. Put a bib on her, use a plastic tablecloth, put newspapers under the highchair if that helps you be more relaxed."

FURTHER READING
Meals Without Squeals,
by Christine Berman
M.P.H, R.D. and Jacki
Fromer, Bull
Publishing Co., 1991.

*Feeding Your Baby
in the Nineties: From
Conception to Age
Two,* by Louise
Lambert-Lagacé,
Stoddart, 1992.

That same relaxed attitude should be kept in mind when your toddler is actually eating (as well as dropping food on the floor). Urging your child to eat, or trying to persuade him to try foods he doesn't want, are rarely productive activities. The best approach seems to be offering small amounts of a variety of foods, and letting your toddler decide how much or how little he needs. As Lynch-Vogelzang sums up the issue: "Parents are responsible for offering their toddlers a variety of nourishing foods, but the toddler is responsible for deciding how much he or she is going to eat of each food. If we can just keep that in mind, we can avoid a lot of mealtime battles."

THE BREASTFED TODDLER: NURSING PAST THE FIRST YEAR

SIXTEEN-MONTH-OLD EVAN has become increasingly cranky over the past 20 minutes. Now he stops banging on the floor with his truck and climbs onto his mother's lap. Lunch was about an hour ago, and he's definitely ready for an afternoon nap. His mother, Jacky Hunt, snuggles him into her arms, lifts the bottom of her T-shirt, and smiles as he sighs contentedly. Ten minutes later he's sound asleep, a trickle of milk at the corner of his mouth. Nursing has worked its magic again.

Jacky remembers that when her oldest daughter, Kristen, now ten, became a nursing toddler, she often received negative comments. "People often said to me then 'Is she *still* nursing?'" Jacky says. "But now that's changed. Now they're more likely to say 'Oh, how lovely, I wish I'd been able to nurse that long.' I'm really seeing a change in attitude."

Part of that change in attitude has resulted from continuing research into the benefits of breastfeeding. While at one time the nutritional and immunological attributes of breastmilk were thought to be insignificant after the first six to twelve months, new research shows that the benefits continue as long as the nursing does. In fact, research has found that the concentration of antibodies in breastmilk actually increases in the second year.

A 1991 study looked at children breastfed up to three years of age and found the overall rate of illness throughout that time was significantly lower than for children not breastfed. And several studies in the late 1980s showed that ear infections are much less common in breastfed toddlers. The protection breastfeeding provides against illness can be particularly valuable for the toddler who is in group daycare. Breastmilk is also easily digested and may be the only food a sick child can tolerate; continued nursing will help him recover more quickly.

Other benefits of breastfeeding past the first year include better development of the jaw and dental arch (because of the different sucking technique used while nursing), meaning the child is less likely to need orthodontic work or to have speech problems in later years. It also continues to benefit the allergic child, providing a longer time for him to develop tolerance for other foods.

Jacky firmly believes that continued nursing has kept Evan healthy. "With the older two in school, Evan is constantly exposed to cold germs and other viruses, but he's rarely sick and always recovers quickly if he does get a runny nose or mild cold."

But that isn't the benefit that comes to mind first when you ask Jacky why she feels nursing Evan is important. To her, the emotional aspects of nursing—the things that can't be measured in research studies—are what keep her committed to their breastfeeding relationship.

"There are hundreds of benefits, just hundreds of them. But I think most of all, it makes both Evan and me happier. Nursing helps keep his frustration in check," she says. "If he's having a temper tantrum, nursing is the one thing that always calms him down. And it calms the mother down too. When he starts screaming about some little thing, I feel like screaming too—but nursing brings us both out of it. He relaxes, I relax, we start over."

Jacky also finds that continued nursing helps her to maintain an unpressured approach to Evan's eating. He eats a variety of solid foods, and drinks juice and water from a baby cup, but, like all toddlers, has

ETIQUETTE FOR NURSING TODDLERS

Because breastfeeding past the first year is unusual in our society, mothers often feel they want to use a little more discretion when nursing their older babies in public, especially if they face disapproval from friends or relatives. A couple of suggestions:

- You may want to teach your little one a code word for nursing that will not be recognized when he shouts it out in a public place. Babies often develop their own term, often a variation on nursing such as "num-nums," and others use related words such as "side" (from hearing Mom say, "Want the other side?"). As early as possible, start using the word you want your toddler to use.
- A toddler can also learn to wait when nursing on the spot is not convenient. Many mothers gradually start setting limits on where and when they nurse, using phrases like "when we get home," or "when we get to the [parked!] car." It might help to carry alternatives like juice or crackers with you when introducing new "nursing rules."
- When you need bolstering against an insensitive remark, consider this lovely thought, passed on by mother and past board chair of La Leche League Shirley Phillips: "Someone from outside, looking at a nursing toddler, sees the emerging child: the legs dangling over the mother's lap, the long hair. But the mother, looking down into her toddler's eyes, sees the baby still within."

days when he seems uninterested in food. On those days, Jacky doesn't worry. She's confident that the nutritional value of her milk will keep him going. Toddler nursing has its share of surprises, too. Jacky had expected that as her baby grew older, he'd nurse less frequently, but that hasn't been the case. Evan was a relatively infrequent nurser as an infant, but Jacky estimates that he now nurses between ten and fifteen times a day. While many toddlers do nurse only once or twice a day at Evan's age, each toddler's nursing pattern is unique.

Jacky points out that many of these are what she calls "touch nursings"—"just three or four sucks and he's off my lap again." Many are for comfort, when he's fallen and bumped his head, or become frustrated with some task he can't quite accomplish. Longer nursings tend to be at naptime or bedtime, or when Jacky's been out for a while and returns, a time when he needs to re-establish their relationship.

It's that relationship that Jacky thinks about when she discusses weaning. The weaning process began, of course, almost a year ago, when Evan first started eating solid foods and drinking from a cup, but it's hard to predict when it will end. "I don't know when Evan will stop nursing," she says. "When you're in the middle of it, it's almost impossible to imagine a time when he won't be, even though I know it will happen one day. All I'm sure of is that he still needs it now. He's not yet ready to break that bond with me."

TOILET TIME?: WHEN AND HOW TO INTRODUCE THE POTTY

N O MORE DIAPERS. Whether that means no more diapers to wash or no more diapers to buy, it sounds good to most parents. Unfortunately, in between full-time diapers and no more diapers lies "toilet training"—a period of puddles on the floor, poop in the pant-legs, and frantic dashes from the grocery line to the washroom. Is there an easy way?

Patricia O'Manique, of Canadian Mothercraft in Ottawa (a non-profit childcare and parent-support organization), is the head teacher in their intermediate (ages two to three) daycare room. "We've trained hundreds of children here!" she says, laughing.

At Mothercraft they use what O'Manique calls a "natural" approach to training, waiting until each child is ready. "This is a complex skill involving many different steps," she explains. "Most children are two and a half, or even three, before they are ready to consistently use the toilet." For reasons unknown, girls often graduate from diapers a little earlier than boys: a reassuring phenomenon to keep in mind if yours is the only boy on the block!

At Mothercraft, when a child seems ready to start (see sidebar on the next page for signs to watch for), the staff begin by introducing the toilet or potty. Many experts suggest that a low, stable potty feels more comfortable and secure to small children. (Some come with "urine guards" for boys which are quite sharp and could really hurt a child who sat down a bit crooked, so take the guard off and teach him to hold his penis down.) There's no pressure to actually *use* the toilet; staff just suggest after each diaper change that the child try sitting on it. Later, the casual invitation to try to pee in it can be added, preferably when the diaper has been dry for a while and the child probably needs to go.

"You could also read a little story about the toilet, and talk about how he is learning to use the toilet like a big boy, but I wouldn't make a big deal out of it," suggests O'Manique.

Young toddlers are more or less oblivious to what's going on in their diaper. So the first step in successful toilet learning is awareness of what the sensations of elimination mean. Parents can help with this by casually commenting to a child who is, for example, obviously having a b.m., "Oh, you're having a poop. When you're finished we'll change your diaper so you're nice and clean." Later, you can help her connect the "warning signs" with what happens next: "You look squirmy. Maybe you have to go to the bathroom?" A practical tip: the superabsorbent disposable diapers don't ever feel very wet; if your child doesn't seem to know or care if she's wet or not, you might try a less efficient diaper that doesn't hold urine so comfortably!

If you're comfortable with it, leaving the bathroom door open when *you're* on the toilet, and talking to your toddler about what you're

---

SIGNS OF READINESS FOR TOILET LEARNING
Watch for the following signs that your child may be ready to begin using the toilet:

- **Her diapers are dry for long stretches of time.**
- **She understands that her urine and bowel movements are the result of her own elimination, is aware of when she has a wet or dirty diaper, and (ideally) prefers to be dry and clean.**
- **She understands that bigger children and grown-ups use the toilet instead of diapers, and that she will do the same one day.**
- **She talks about it—perhaps asking to be changed, wondering where the "flush" goes on the big toilet, or even asking to try it out.**
- **She will be more in control of the process if she can pull down her own pants and sit on the potty. (Loose track pants are much easier to manage than those cute overalls.)**

IN LESS THAN A DAY?

The book *Toilet Training in Less than a Day* has been snapped up by thousands of parents eager to get the whole messy process over with quickly. The method (to crudely summarize) involves spending an entire day with your child (and a doll) doing little but drinking, peeing and rewarding. After this intensive teaching session, the child will supposedly be "trained."

Is this a reasonable way to teach a child to use the toilet? Patricia O'Manique of Canadian Mothercraft doesn't think so. "I think this approach puts too much pressure on parent and child both," she says. "We see some children who are pushed too quickly into using the toilet, and they may stay dry for a few days but they often lose it again."

Think about other self-care skills your toddler is learning, like dressing or feeding himself. Would you expect him to master these tasks in a day? Using the toilet involves not only mechanical skills but a sustained mental awareness—recognizing when you need to stop playing and go to the potty—which kids usually develop gradually, with practice.

doing, can really help. Children are natural imitators and babies with older siblings generally know all about toilets. It's certainly the most natural way to learn a skill—imagine trying to drive a car without ever having seen it done!

O'Manique stresses that at Mothercraft they never force a child to sit on the toilet. If a child resists the idea altogether, or doesn't seem to be "catching on" after a couple of weeks, the subject is dropped. "It's better to try again in a few months," she suggests. "When children are pushed too hard, it becomes a very unpleasant and discouraging experience, and they are likely to resist the toilet instead of being eager to learn. In the end, it also takes longer."

Penelope Leach suggests that parents minimize discouraging accidents at first by leaving the child in diapers until he's using the potty fairly frequently. Even then, diapers can be returned to for naps, outings, or on rushed days when you just can't face puddles; just make sure that you don't make the diapers seem like a failure or punishment. Virtually all experts stress that scolding or shaming a child for the inevitable accidents is harmful (as well as unfair). Quiet encouragement is more appropriate: "Oh-oh, did you wet your pants? We'll give you nice dry ones and next time I bet you can use your potty to pee."

In fact, some experts suggest you not make *too* big a deal about successes, either. Of course you will cheer his accomplishment, but Dr. Marianne Neifert, author of *Dr. Mom*, warns that "offering treats or promoting the idea that he is pleasing you or someone else by his behaviour will not be as successful as his learning to use the toilet because he wants to." A warm "Good for you!" allows him to feel proud of *himself*.

It's a subtle but important difference. Reminds Leach, "Toilet training is not a question of making a child do something *for you*. It is a matter of helping him do something *for himself*."

At Home with Your Toddler:
Living with Toddler Traits

Brenda Cooke

PEOPLE THINK OF INFANCY as the "high maintenance" stage of parenting, but we'd vote for toddlerhood. Yes, babies are more helpless and needier, but they don't smear your lipstick all over the mirror, or struggle and scream when it's time to go home, or suddenly dart into the parking lot. "Vigilance" and "patience" are key qualities for parents of toddlers—and sheer physical stamina doesn't hurt, either!

Experienced parents and professionals alike observe that life with a toddler is easier on everybody if we accept and plan around his limitations, rather than trying to force him to behave with more self-control and maturity than he can manage. Minimizing frustrations and safety hazards, building in extra time for transitions, and respecting his own individual temperament and pace of development will pay off in less conflict, less stress for you—and more fun together.

Yet life goes on, and it doesn't always suit your toddler's preferences. Helping him to cope with the many limits and demands in his life is sometimes a real challenge. He *has* to have his immunization; he *can't* play in the toilet; you simply *must* get to the bank, even though it's naptime. At these times it's all too easy to become frustrated and annoyed with his demands and protests, even to feel that he's deliberately making things difficult for you. But he's not. He's really too immature even to understand your feelings and needs, and his own view of the world is simply the only one he is aware of right now.

It's not easy to summon the energy to play finger-games with your toddler in the check-out line, when you're just as fed up and sick of waiting as he is; or to jump up from the couch to take him away from the fireplace and find something enticing for him to do, when you really want to read the paper; or to play the same old "bears in a cave" game for the hundredth time. Parents ain't perfect, and you won't always rise to these challenges the way you'd like to. But that's okay. Your child is both resilient and forgiving—he'll give you many, many chances to do better. Extend the same generosity to him, and you'll both do just fine.

LOVING LIMITS: POSITIVE DISCIPLINE, TODDLER-STYLE

N THE FIRST YEAR, WE RARELY THINK of the limits we set for our babies as "discipline." We keep them safe, we prevent them from damaging things, but we don't expect them to understand our rules or to change their behaviour accordingly. In toddlerhood, though, our children start to understand language, and to imitate our actions. They become more aware of other people, more interested in how things are done. They also—perhaps more to the point—develop a formidably strong will, which is frequently in opposition to our own. It's time to begin the long job of teaching our children "how to behave." But how do you teach a toddler?

With very young children, discipline tends to be a "hands-on" process. No, we're not talking about spanking! Rather, we're talking about how parents can physically "help" toddlers, who are simply too young to have developed much self-control, to follow important rules. Here's one example:

Jeff and Max are in the sandbox together, and 18-month-old Jeff has decided it's just fascinating how the wind blows the sand when he throws it into the air. Trouble is, it's blowing straight towards Max. Their mother, Kelly, intervenes.

Hurrying over to the children, she crouches down beside Jeff, holding his arm so that he can't grab another handful. "Jeff." Slightly startled, Jeff looks up. "Don't throw the sand. It could hurt Max's eyes."

"No throw," repeats Jeff, and Kelly takes a step back, watching. Jeff takes an experimental handful, and trickles it into his pie plate. He looks at his mother, who smiles. "That's right, honey."

And now, the crunch. Jeff grabs two fistfuls of sand and flings them, right at his older brother. Luckily, Max has seen it coming and ducked; he has sand in his hair, but he's unhurt. What now?

Kelly doesn't wait for an encore. She scoops Jeff up and has him sitting on a park bench before the dust even settles. Not until after she's got Jeff safely away from the sandbox does she repeat her rule: "Jeff, you can't throw sand. It's not safe." Kelly is crouched in front of Jeff, effectively getting his attention and blocking his escape at the same time. "Now. Let's find something else to do. How about a swing?"

YOUR TODDLER DISCIPLINE TOOL-BOX
Your most effective discipline tools at this age involve prevention.
• **Babyproofing**
• **Careful supervision**
• **Distraction**
• **Enough food, sleep, exercise and attention**

When setting limits with toddlers:
• **Remove them from the trouble**
• **Use simple language**
• **Offer an acceptable alternative, and help them get involved in it**
• **Stay close to prevent a recurrence**

That's an approach parent educator Kathy Lynn approves of. "Toddlers don't have the willpower or the understanding to follow verbal directions consistently. They need us to follow through with action. That helps them understand what we mean, and also that we really *do* mean it!"

"Action" does not mean anger or punishment, though. "It's appropriate to start teaching toddlers that there are limits," notes Lynn, "but it's important not to expect too much. Toddlers are insatiably curious. They are driven to assert their independence. They are ruled by their emotions." So they *will* explore everything they can get their hands on, act defiant, and pitch fits when they don't get their own way. Rather than seeing these inevitable events as "misbehaviour," Lynn suggests, parents do better to understand that "toddlers need to be this way in order to reach the next level of development."

Because toddlers have such poor impulse control, Lynn stresses that prevention is really the most effective discipline "method": "A safe, appropriate physical and social environment, so that toddlers have lots of opportunities to explore and play without getting into trouble, is the first step." Alert supervision, needless to say, is also essential. "Those times when the kids are playing in another room, and your radar is starting to go off but you think to yourself, 'I just need another five minutes so I can finish this thing I'm doing,' *that's* the time to move in and redirect them, before things blow up," says Lynn, laughing. So listen to your parent early warning system!

When it comes to rules and limits, "we need to get really clear ourselves on what is the bottom line, what *has* to happen, and what *can't* happen, and concentrate on those really important issues," suggests Lynn.

Maria Shuwera, mother of Anna (two) and Bastian (four), and a former home daycare provider, agrees: "You have to pick your battles—is this worth the effort and conflict? Before I had kids, I had a lot of plants. Then Bastian came along and he *could not* keep out of them. I moved them up higher and higher, and eventually I got rid of them. I can have plants again in a few years, but I'm not going to get my kids' babyhoods again. I had to ask myself, 'What's really important here?'"

Lynn stresses that enforcing limits with toddlers requires a lot of hands-on guidance: "We're so imbued with the idea of good communication, but parents get into trouble when they expect to reason at length with a toddler, and have that be enough. We need to remember how little they really are." Although some older toddlers can talk quite well, their thought processes are still very immature. Even if they can follow our reasoning, words don't have much immediacy for them. "But if, on the other hand, every time he throws his cup it gets put away, that's a clear message he can begin to understand," explains Lynn.

Does this mean we shouldn't explain rules to our toddlers? Not at all. "You do tell them the rules, because you're starting a learning process," says Lynn. "As you're carrying him away, you say, 'The rule is we don't hurt other people, so I'm taking you away from your sister.'"

YOUR TODDLER'S LIMITS

Parents who expect "big kid" behaviour from their toddler are in for a frustrating year or two. Here's why:

- Toddlers are impulsive. Self-control is a difficult skill. Think how you have to struggle with yourself sometimes not to eat that second brownie. A toddler may "know" she's not supposed to touch—but she still needs your help to overcome that strong urge.
- Toddlers can't understand complex ideas. If you told him last week not to go on the road, will he know you meant this week and next week, too? Does he know exactly what a road is? Does he realize that you mean *any* road, not just the one in front of your apartment building? Rules may seem simple to us—but not to him.
- Toddlers have inconsistent memory and attention. Maybe she remembers the rule: don't go on the road. She remembers it until she sees the dog on the other side—and then she remembers that she loves dogs! It's hard for her to hold both those ideas in her head at the same time.

Of course we still have to set limits for our toddlers, for both safety and sanity's sake. But it's also important to understand that at this age, they really can't help most of their "misbehaviour."

Start offering simple choices, too, recommends Lynn. "Limits on behaviour should go hand-in-hand with choices. Gradually, in the years to come, you shift more control over to them. But right now, you're just introducing the idea: 'It's time for bed. Do you want to walk upstairs with me, or should I carry you?' " Again, this is getting you both started on a path you'll be walking throughout his childhood.

Maria confesses to "going a little overboard" explaining rules to her kids, but she says, "I want them to know why it's not okay. They may not get it at first, but a few months later they do understand." Still, she often finds she has to "act first, and talk later." "With Anna, the point is easily lost. The other day she almost crossed the road by herself. I scooped her up as she stepped out onto the pavement, and she was just furious at being thwarted, totally freaking out. It would have been useless to talk to her then. But later, when she was ready to hear, I reminded her about the rule and how dangerous the street was."

These years are very demanding ones for parents. Just keeping toddlers (and whatever they come into contact with) safe requires vigilance, perseverance and creativity. Their behaviour can be provocative, even dismaying, yet they need our nurturing and positive encouragement as much as they need our limits. And sometimes our efforts to teach those limits seem to be falling into some kind of black hole, with no visible effect.

But have patience. Your toddler's behaviour really will even out with time, as the internal controls so flamboyantly lacking now begin to develop. Maria recalls, "Bastian went through a phase of biting other children, and I just agonized about it. I kept thinking, 'Why is he doing this?' But sometimes there *is* no 'why.' After a while, the biting simply stopped. He grew out of it—just like he grew out of trying to eat my plants."

"DON'T TOUCH!": THE NEED TO EXPLORE

INDY AND JEFF ARE MUSICIANS, and their instruments are important to them. Jeff's expensive guitar is displayed precariously on a stand in the living room, easily accessible when the urge to play is felt. It's also accessible to their one-year-old son, who is drawn to it like a magnet.

This couple has decided not to move their guitar or most of their other belongings to protect them from little Willy. Instead, they slap his hand and tell him "*No!*" many times a day. "This is our home, and these are our things," explains Jeff. "Willy is going to have to learn to respect our home."

Kathy Lynn takes issue with this kind of thinking. "Where is Willy's home?" she asks. "Everyone has a right to feel comfortable and competent in their own home, not just adults. And when the needs of a young child conflict with those of the parents, I would argue that the adults should be the more adaptable. Children aren't little for long, but for that short period, their needs come first."

Do toddlers really *need* to touch things? "It's not an exaggeration to say it's their job," says Lynn. "They learn by touching, tasting, and handling things, not by being careful. They thrive in an environment that offers them as many ways as possible to explore their world safely."

A child-friendly home doesn't limit a child's exploration to the toy box, says Lynn. "I like to see posters put way down low on the wall, at child's-eye height." (Laminating them will keep them fairly indestructible.) "There should be cupboards or drawers the child *can* get into, say where plastic bowls and containers are kept, and books that she's free to handle and explore, stored at her level."

Lynn suggests some other features of a child-friendly home:

"SHE'S WRECKING MY STUFF!": YOUR OLDER CHILD

"It was wonderful how well my four-year-old accepted the new baby," recalls mother of two Janetta Valenti. "He was so tender and protective—until she got up on her feet!"

It's a common story. Just when your older child is at the stage where he wants his art, construction projects, and treasures to be preserved for eternity, your baby is at the stage where she wants to smush, crumple, eat or knock down everything she can get her hands on.

Of course you will urge big brother to be tolerant, explain that she doesn't know any better, and protect her from his wrath. But try to protect him, too. His latest painting is at least as precious to him as your cut-glass vase is to you—and he *won't* always remember to put it out of reach. How can you help?

- The fridge door is no longer a safe display area. Can you hang a high bulletin board for his pictures, or tape them along the top of a window or sliding glass door?
- If he has his own room, consider making it off-limits for your toddler, except under your watchful eye. Encourage your older child to close his door if he needs to, and then help by distracting the toddler when she wails in outrage on the other side. If they share a room, you might put some high shelving along one wall, or install shelving in the closet and make that space his for now—but help him remember to keep it closed.
- Give him a babyproof "treasure box," maybe even with a lock and key, for gum wrappers, cards, crab claws, etc.
- Find ways to include the toddler in family play. But try also to find a bit of time alone with just your oldest, so you can play cards or a board game, or work on a painting together, undisturbed.

R_x FOR VISITING
TODDLERS
Visiting with an active
toddler can be a special
challenge, and Kathy
Lynn has some sugges-
tions to protect your
child and "foreign envi-
ronments" from each
other:

- Avoid hunger, fatigue,
  and pent-up energy—
  factors that lead to distressing behaviour in
  children (and grown-
  ups!). An active child is
  less likely to wreak
  havoc at Grandma's if
  you stop off at the
  playground on the way.
- If possible, ask your
  hosts if you may put
  the most obviously
  enticing and break-
  able/dangerous things
  out of reach.
- Bring toys and activi-
  ties for your child to
  do.
- Supervise closely, even
  though you'd really
  prefer to just sit on the
  couch and chat.
- Keep it short!

The home is thoroughly babyproofed, so she is safe and not constantly tempted by objects she can't have and areas she can't enter. (Of course she can't have free access to your office or work-shop, but the main living areas are open to her.)

She can reach most of her own toys and clothes, and put them away easily, too. There is a consistent place for her things, so she knows where to find what she wants.

She is allowed to enjoy messy activities now and then, and there is a place (the kitchen floor?) where she can do this without leaving indelible stains.

Her environment has been modified to help her function competently: a step-stool in the bathroom so she can reach to wash her hands, a potty on the ground floor so she can "get there" in time, "finger foods" so she can feed herself, etc.

As Jeff and Cindy have discovered, teaching tod-dlers to respect property is also very hard work. One-year-olds, says Lynn, are just not develop-mentally ready to distinguish consistently between objects they may and may not touch. "It's like trying to toilet train an infant, because she'll have to learn it eventually," says Lynn. "It just makes the process longer and more unpleas-ant for everyone."

Obviously, we can't eliminate every danger in our child's environment, and children *do* eventually need to learn to respect limits. Lynn says that what we say to our toddlers as we restrict their exploration starts the learning process. "Even with a well-babyproofed house, there will be many times we have to 'redirect' young children," she says. "We can teach and distract them at the same time, by saying 'This is not a toy' as we take away an object, and saying 'Here is a toy to play with' as we offer them an alternative. Similarly, we can teach them the words that mean danger: 'This is *hot*...It hurts to touch it.' 'Knives are *dangerous*. They can hurt you.'" The one-year-old who murmurs "ot" as he reaches for the oven will one day be a three-year-old who automatically stands clear when you open the door.

"I was putting in the laundry while my two-year-old played in the living room," recalls Susan Newman. "I was gone maybe ten minutes. When I came back, Joe was gone, but his trail was plain to see. He had pulled a chair over to the wall, climbed up, and lifted down my purse from a hook. He had opened my purse, pulled out my keys, and got the front door open. I found him in the car, trying to get the key in the ignition! I would not have believed it possible."

But children this young cannot be depended on to consistently follow the rules. Even a two-year-old who can explain perfectly why he should never touch the toaster can be overwhelmed by the urge to stick a spoon down the toaster slot. "Once they're mobile, they need to be supervised," says Lynn. "That's the bottom line."

THE KAMIKAZE TODDLER

All toddlers need to explore and touch. But in some toddlers, that drive seems to be relentless. Determined, persistent and endlessly curious, these are the children who scale the living-room bookshelf before their second birthday (better bolt it to the wall!), figure out how to open a child-resistant safety cap in about ten minutes (lock up your medications!), and just *know* that the coolest things in the house are up on the counter (one little boy we know used to say, "Lift me up. I want to see what I can get...."). Their parents soon become the most ingenious babyproofers alive, and live, for these hectic two years, in houses that are battened down like ships.

What drives toddlers to explore their world with such ferocious and single-minded intensity? And why do some toddlers seem content (most of the time) to explore within the boundaries set by their parents and caregivers, while others constantly push against those same boundaries?

"We used to think that all children were born pretty much equal, and that their personalities developed as a result of the environment they were raised in," comments Sue Martin, a professor of early childhood education at Toronto's Centennial College who specializes in infant and toddler development. "Now we see that they really are complex little individuals right from birth, with their own temperamental characteristics. And research is showing that temperament tends to remain constant, even into adulthood. Children's personality development will, of course, be affected by their experience. But those basic personality traits—whether easygoing, or intense, or slow to warm up—do persist."

So, the good news is that your little holy terror isn't like that because of anything you did wrong, he's just made that way. And the bad news is he's *always* going to be like that?!? Before you panic, remember: this personality trait looks a lot different in an older child or adult. Your kamikaze toddler is absolutely determined to explore and understand his world, in his own way. Right now, he lacks the judgement and experience to do this safely, but it's an admirable trait in itself. Persistence, self-determination, curiosity—these are qualities needed by people who achieve great things. As your child matures, you'll be glad to see his many strengths. In the meantime, batten down the hatches!

HOME FROM DAYCARE: THE ROCKY REUNION

....

IT'S BEEN A LONG DAY AT WORK, and a long time away from your little one. Soon, though, you'll be together again, and you'll be so glad to see each other. Visions of a lovely evening together fill your head: a big hug when you pick her up at daycare, laughing chatter on the car ride home, a pleasant family dinner...

Well, it's a nice dream. It might even come true. But what if your after-daycare reunion looks more like the following real-life examples:

Elaine lets herself into her caregiver's back yard and watches her daughter dig contentedly in the big sandbox. Unearthing a prize, Sarah turns to show her caregiver—and catches sight of her mom. But instead of the hoped-for welcoming smile, Sarah's face suddenly dissolves into frantic sobs. She races for her mother, climbs up to her neck, and cowers against her. "That's funny," remarks the caregiver. "She's had a really good time today."

When Rita arrives at the daycare, her son Connor is skidding around on a ride-on truck. "Hi, Connor!" she enthuses. Connor favours her with a glance, returns to his ride. "C'mon, honey, time to go home," she tries. He scoots away. Rita gives him a little more playtime, then walks over. "Okay, big guy, we have to go now. Here, I'll give you a boost." She bends down and picks Connor up. His feet lock around the truck. Stuck with the whole unwieldy contraption in the air, Rita's not sure what to do next. Try as she might, she can't dislodge the truck. It takes the combined efforts of Rita and a staff member to separate Connor from his vehicle. By the time the two of them make it outside, Rita is thoroughly embarrassed and Connor is furious.

Sam knocks on the door, and finds Jason packed up and ready to go. But still he can't seem to make a "clean getaway." Jason kicks off his boots, yanks off the mitts. "Too hot! No boots!" There's a flurry of collecting, a struggle that ends with Sam carrying Jason in stocking feet. In the car, there's a show-down over where to put the still-wet painting Jason insists on clutching to his chest; back home, more "senseless" conflicts leave Sam feeling inadequate and exhausted. How come Jason always seems so co-operative with their daycare provider, while Sam can't even get a pair of boots on him?

First of all, says family childcare provider Marguerite Townrow, it might help to know that "almost every child has some sort of 're-entry' trouble at one time or another." Townrow, who is education co-ordinator for the South Fraser [B.C.] Family Child Care Association, notes that "toddlers often have a tough time handling transitions, anyway. And at the end of the day, when blood sugar is low and fatigue is high, they 'lose it' easily. I've seen toddlers start kicking, screaming and hitting at pick-up time, and I've also seen, at the other end of the spectrum, a kind of clingy, 'rag-doll' reaction: 'I've been very self-sufficient all day but now I'm helpless!'"

As Alicia Lieberman explains in her book, *The Emotional Life of the Toddler*, "toddlers often do not show pleasure on being picked up at the end of the day. They may be involved in play and figure that the parent can wait for them for a change. They may be angry at the separation and show it through a 'cold shoulder' or through outright aggression. They may have intense positive and negative emotions raging inside them and try to cope with these feelings by keeping some distance from the parents until they can offer a genuinely warm hello."

Normal or not, this kind of response is no fun for the parent. So Townrow has some ideas for smoothing out those bumpy reunions:

Have a predictable routine. "When the parents arrive at pretty much the same time every day, the child gets to know when to expect them and that's easier," says Townrow. "When that's not possible, it can help if the parent calls before leaving work, so that the child can be prepared for their arrival."

Wind down at the end of the day. Skilled caregivers often move to "low-intensity" activities in the late afternoon, so the kids are not overexcited when the parents arrive. Another good strategy, weather permitting, suggests Townrow, is to have the children outside at the end of the day—thus eliminating one whole step at pick-up time.

Greet the child first. "Sometimes the parents come in and start talking to me right away, and then you get a kind of jealous or possessive acting-out from the child," observes Townrow. Even if your child is ignoring you, he should get a clear message that he is first on your priority list.

Have a snack in the car. The commute home is often much pleasanter if your child (and maybe you?) can munch on an apple, some dry cereal or cheese and crackers. And then, since you won't all be starving, you can take a few minutes to read a story or play together before diving into dinner preparations at home.

Finally, it's important not to take a toddler's ups and downs—at any time—too personally. It's easy to feel, as one mother did, that "he's doing this to punish me for leaving him." But there is another way of looking at it. Most children, of all ages, seem to save their most intense feelings and behaviour for their parents. Even toddlers will try to "hold it together" at daycare. They play, and laugh, and cry, but not, perhaps, with the abandon we see at home. In *Touchpoints* (Addison-Wesley, 1992), developmental paediatrician T. Berry Brazelton explains it like this: "They store up their powerful reactions for the reunion at the end of the day." Throughout children's lives, their more extreme and difficult behaviour tends to be directed towards their parents. It's not because we're inept at managing our children—it's because, in a healthy family, the parents are the "safe haven" where children can regress, let their hair down, and express their scariest emotions.

So she's not acting that way because she hates you. Maybe she's even acting that way because she *loves* you so strongly. Hang on to that thought, while time works its magic. As she grows out of her "toddler turbulence," and feels more confident about her separations from you, both hellos and goodbyes will become easier.

A NEW BABY!: HELPING YOUR TODDLER
MAKE ROOM FOR NUMBER TWO

T THE TENDER AGE OF 18 MONTHS, Shane became a big brother to baby Cody. It wasn't a complete shock. His parents had talked about the new baby growing in his mom's belly, and let him feel it. But as his mother, Marla VanLuven, says, "at 18 months there's not a lot you can do to prepare a kid. He was hardly talking."

Is it traumatic for a toddler to adjust to a new baby in the family? Parents who have realistic expectations and help to smooth the way are often pleasantly surprised at how easily their older baby takes a sibling in stride.

"He basically jumped right in and handled it well," says Marla, whose two boys are now seven and 25 months. "He doesn't really remember ever being without Cody."

Ann Bolton, whose three children (Julie, Scott and Eric) were each born 19 months apart, agrees that there is often little you can do to prepare the older child. "With Julie it was different. She was already talking quite well. We read *The New Baby*, by Mercer Mayer, and I don't know if she really believed it but she learned to say, 'Baby in Mommy's tummy.' We could explain to her what new babies were like and how to handle them. But Scott wouldn't sit down long enough to read a book. It was basically a shock for him when Erik arrived."

Ann feels the hardest part for her children was the separation from her while she was in hospital: "That was really hard on them, both times." Marla had a slightly different problem. She wasn't even away overnight, so Shane hardly had time to miss her—but she was also dealing with an active toddler just a day after giving birth. "On that first day I was nursing Cody, and Shane wanted me, too. Then my mom came over and took him out to play, and that was just what he needed."

In fact, most parents agree that the main adjustment the older baby has to make is getting used to less "mommy time," and that it's wise to enlist the help of dads and other familiar people who can pay some extra attention to the firstborn. Gifts, too, are not amiss. Even a one-year-old can notice that there's a heap of presents arriving and none of them is for her. Ann even bought "birthday" presents for her older children and said they were from the new baby.

"We always took the attitude that this was their baby, too," says Ann. "Toddlers have a real fascination with babies, and we encouraged that by showing them how to touch the baby gently or check out his toes." Child development expert Penelope Leach advises parents to nurture this early interest by helping the child feel that the baby likes her. Remark on how the baby smiles so much at her, or how he stopped crying when she rocked his carriage, and be tactful about the times when her clumsy advances backfire.

Both families have found that a regular routine becomes more important with two (or more) young ones—it not only makes things more manageable for the parents, but gives the children a sense of security in the midst of all the changes. Marla says, "Getting into a daily routine is the smartest thing I ever did. For example, we have rest time every afternoon for at least an hour. Shane may not always sleep, but it's a quiet time for all of us." Marla is also glad they decided to acquire a second crib rather than rush Shane out of his: "We've always put Shane to bed while he's still awake, and then he settles himself down to sleep. That's easier to maintain when he can't get out of bed."

Child development expert Penelope Leach suggests it's wise to introduce any *other* changes in the older child's life well in advance of the birth. If you need her crib for the baby, try to move her into a big bed a couple of months beforehand. If you're still nursing him and aren't willing to breastfeed two at once (which can be done, by the way), then it's only fair to wean him gradually over the pregnancy so it doesn't seem the baby has stolen "his" breasts.

BABY SPACING: HOW DOES IT AFFECT THE CHILDREN?
Theories abound as to the "ideal" spacing of kids. The reality is, though, that children are born as close together as ten months, and as far apart as ten years—and we parents don't always have complete control over Mother Nature's timing!

Does it make any difference to children if they are closely spaced? It depends, believes paediatrician T. Berry Brazelton, on how it is for the parents. He writes in *Toddlers and Parents*: "I am convinced that the time between children is not very important to the children of a family, but it certainly is to the parents . . . if parents can tolerate the pressures of each new child, and keep a margin of energy to enjoy each child, all the children will be likely to thrive."

Coping with the needs of two babies can be overwhelming, but Ann observes that her older children seem to have become a little more self-sufficient than many kids their age. She says wryly, "They learn pretty fast that if they want to play outside and I'm breastfeeding the baby, it will be a shorter wait if they can start getting into their own snowsuits."

Still, she cautions against expecting overly mature behaviour: "There's a tendency to want them to act older than they are." Marla agrees: "I have to remind myself that Shane is still a baby himself." Beside a newborn, your little one suddenly looks huge and your patience with her typical toddler behaviour may plummet. But Dr. Marianne Neifert, paediatrician and author of *Dr. Mom*, advises: "During the period of adjustment after the baby's birth, try to loosen up expectations and standards for toddlers and other children." In fact, it's quite common for a toddler to revert to *more* babyish behaviour; try to respond to this as the plea for love and attention it is.

There's no doubt that, in the short term at least, two babies add up to parental fatigue. "It's really hard work in the early days," says Ann. "You just plan to be exhausted." Single-parent outings and dinner preparation become especially difficult. But both moms are clearly enjoying their little ones, too. Says Ann, "These are incredibly special times, the times of which memories are made." Marla concurs. "This is the greatest job I ever had. My kids are both happy kids. And the fun stuff is just beginning."

"LET'S DO IT AGAIN, AND AGAIN, AND AGAIN..." REPETITION AND PERSEVERANCE

EDTIME AT LAST, AND YOUR TODDLER is rubbing her eyes. You pick up three or four library books and ask which one she'd like for a bedtime story. "How about this one about cows? You really liked the cows we saw on Sunday." The bright and tempting illustrations on the cover aren't going to work, though. Your daughter folds her little arms and firmly says: "I want *Go, Dog, Go!*"

Now *Go, Dog, Go!* is a charming book, but you've read it every night for the past five nights and you're getting a little tired of it. Actually, very tired. Why do toddlers want to hear the same story over and over?

Picku Multani's son, Angad, is two, and she says, "It isn't just reading the same book over and over. It's playing the same game over and over the same way—stacking up the blocks and knocking them down, then stacking them up again and knocking them down again."

Many parents might wonder what the appeal is. Pat Tretjack, supervisor of the Sheridan College Childcare Centre in Oakville, Ontario, points out that "toddlers do these things over and over because they need to. They are repeating their behaviours and actions in order to perfect a skill. It's how toddlers learn."

She remembers that her own son would insist she stop the stroller every time they passed someone using a lawnmower. He wanted to watch and figure out what those amazing machines were all about, and he'd get really upset if she just went on by. Eventually, though, he decided he understood lawnmowers and was willing to go for walks without taking lawnmower breaks.

"You can't give in to everything, of course, because children need to

REASSURING ROUTINES

Each morning, two-year-old Melanie awakens early and is brought into her parents' bed for a cuddle. When it's time to get up, she carefully picks up the glasses on the bedside table and hands them to her mother, Alison. One morning, Alison had to go to the bathroom, so she hopped out of bed, grabbed her glasses and headed out of the room. "Melanie just fell apart," Alison remembers. "I couldn't believe how upset she was. It was as though, in her mind, the little ritual with the glasses was the signal that life was unfolding as it should."

A toddler's fondness for repetition isn't limited to playtime: many toddlers seem to love daily routines and rituals. There's no need to be rigid or governed by a clock, but these repeated patterns can help toddlers keep their equilibrium. Routines are especially helpful for handling transition times like saying goodbye at daycare, settling down for nap or bed, or getting through "arsenic hour" (when you need to make dinner, and your tired toddler needs attention). Whether it's having three stories at bedtime, sharing a "hug, kiss and pat" before you head off to work, going for a walk after breakfast, or giving Mom her glasses every morning, routines that you initiate may become rituals your toddler clings to.

Why are they so important? To a young child, the world is a pretty confusing place, full of events that "just happen." By contrast, things that occur in about the same way or at about the same time become familiar and predictable. They make sense out of the jumble of life, and help kids know what to expect. As paediatrician and author William Sears writes, in *The Discipline Book*, "routines give a child a sense of mastery."

learn limits," Tretjack says. "But this is a developmental stage where it's important to let them go through this repetitive learning process as much as possible."

If your child's passion for repetition is driving you nuts, Tretjack suggests that you try to distract and redirect him. Since toddlers tend to be very curious, a new and interesting game or story might just do the trick. Not always, though, because another trait common to many toddlers is persistence. Tretjack explains, "Some kids are more persistent than others. It's part of some children's innate personalities. They won't give in and they won't give up."

Consider Lorraine Black's two-year-old son, Evan. When this little guy decided he wanted to fill a hot-water bottle himself, Lorraine explained that he couldn't because hot water is dangerous. Then she put the water bottle out of reach. Evan seemed mollified and wandered off to play with his toy truck, so Lorraine thought that was that. But minutes later, she saw him standing on his truck, trying to reach the hot-water bottle. Lorraine gently took the truck away and offered him some other toys to play with, and then turned back to her housework. Next thing she knew, Evan was dragging a kitchen chair over to the counter where the water bottle was. "When he wants something, he really wants it!" she says.

Part of what makes the toddler's persistence so challenging is his newly developed capacity for memory. The out-of-sight-out-of-mind trick that worked when he was a baby just won't wash now.

Picku Multani learned this firsthand when Angad fell in love with a big yellow truck while on a family vacation. Because it would have been impossible to bring the vehicle home, Picku had to say no. She tried to distract Angad with offers of other trucks and toys of more manageable sizes, but he would have none of them. "Yellow truck," he insisted.

In the end, there was no other option but to carry her tearful son out of the store and head back to the hotel. Angad talked about "his" yellow truck for the rest of the holiday and during the entire plane trip home. A few weeks later, Picku and her husband were talking while Angad played nearby with his sister, Noor. Picku quietly mentioned a toy she was considering buying for Noor. Immediately Angad rushed over and said, "Toy for Angad? Yellow truck for Angad?"

Picku couldn't believe that he still remembered that yellow truck. "I was even beginning to wonder if it was worth having the truck shipped out here, if it meant that much to him," she says with a laugh.

There are times, though, when a toddler's persistence means, "I really do need to do this." When an apartment-dwelling friend of mine brought her 18-month-old daughter, Lily, over to visit, the little girl was fascinated by our stairs to the second floor. All of our efforts to distract her so that we could sit and talk in the living room failed—she just kept heading back to the stairs. The barrier we set up across the bottom step only added to the allure as she struggled to climb over it on her way up. In the end, we decided that we could chat while sitting on the stairs just as easily as on the couch in the living room, so we spent a very pleasant afternoon catching up *and* helping Lily master her stair climbing.

"Be tolerant when you can," advises Tretjack. "It's all part of the toddler's drive towards independence." And be patient too—that same persistence that can be so challenging now will be a great asset to your child when she grows up.

OUT AND ABOUT: HEADING INTO THE WORLD WITH YOUR TODDLER

HEN WE GATHERED TOGETHER ALL OUR columns about various outings and excursions with toddlers, we found two essential rules:

1) Plan ahead.
2) Find, and patronize, a child-friendly doctor, restaurant, hairdresser, store...

So there you have it. Time your outing to avoid your toddler's hungry and tired times, try to keep it short, pack along emergency supplies (food, clothing and diversions), and avoid places where they aren't nice to kids. Want a little detail? Read on.

Shop till you drop

When it comes to shopping with toddlers, success and disaster are sometimes separated only by sheer luck. Will she get it in her head that she *must* hold the drippy pack of chicken legs, and dissolve into anguished wails when you can't allow it? Will the person ahead of you get into a long dispute about cashing a cheque, and push your child's tolerance for waiting over the edge? We mortals can't control such things. But there *are* ways to increase the odds of a pleasant excursion.

Friday morning means grocery shopping at the Feltham household. Melanie Feltham, who works Monday to Thursday, likes to avoid the Saturday crowds. She and her two young boys (Blake, two, and Morgan, four) have it down to a routine, and it usually goes pretty smoothly.

"We go to the library first, and the boys can each bring one book into the store with them. We always go to the same store, so they know what to expect. We count the aisles—when we get to ten, we're done—and I

A PLEA FOR CHILD-FRIENDLY STORES

Here's a question for retailers, bankers, and restaurateurs: how many sales are missed due to baby-unfriendly merchandising practices?

"I have actually seen a store where all the baby clothing and equipment was down a flight of stairs," says father of three John Barton. "I looked at my stroller, looked at the stairs, and left." Washrooms without change tables (or no washrooms at all), stroller-impassable aisles, rickety (or no) high chairs, and long waits due to too few staff all conspire against completed business. On the other hand, we know a little video store with a box of toys in the corner that gets grateful return business, despite its limited selection, from parents who are actually able to browse with a toddler in tow.

tell them what they can choose: like, 'When we get to the cereal aisle, you can pick one.'"

Melanie deals with long waits at the checkout by having something for the kids to do. "I'll pack along juice or snacks, or open a box of crackers I'm buying. Or this is when they can look at their new books. Sometimes there's something unbreakable at the checkout, like little plastic dinosaurs, that I'll let them 'borrow' while we wait. But I never buy anything at the checkout display. They don't freak out about the candy, because they know it just won't happen."

John Barton, who does most of the shopping for his family with a toddler in tow, is home most days and so has a more flexible schedule. "I tend to go a few times a week so no one trip lasts too long. That way, it's an outing, not an endurance trial. We usually have fun," John reflects. "At the grocery store, we talk about what we're getting. Jackie likes to hold the list, and at the checkout, she gets in the cart and helps unload the stuff. She likes to hand over the money, too."

Jackie is an active toddler who doesn't take well to prolonged confinement in a stroller. "At the mall, it's best if I don't have to hurry," says John. "She likes to walk between stores, and sit on every bench we pass.

SHOPPING SAFETY

It can happen so quickly. You need to have a good look at that snowsuit before you buy it, so you tell your toddler to "stay close" and start checking out zippers and cuffs. Suddenly, you look around and realize he's nowhere in sight! Now what?

- Nine times out of ten, your panic will be momentary. Call his name, and say "Answer me!" Take a quick dash around the aisles, then drop to your knees and check under the clothes racks (they make very enticing hidey-holes). If you don't find him right away, enlist a clerk to help.
- As your toddler gets older, he will learn to stay within a safe distance, and you can also teach him how to get help if you do get separated. But for now, the bottom line is that this is all up to you. Unless he's in a stroller or backpack, in a harness or holding your hand, *you* need to stay close to *him*.
- Shopping carts pose a greater danger than kidnapping! Hospital emergency rooms regularly see injuries resulting from toddlers falling out of grocery carts. Toddlers are much safer in shopping cart seats that are equipped with seat belts or harnesses, and you may want to buy or make your own restraint for times when these are not available. Even so, it's essential to stay close to the cart and alert to your child at all times.

So we sit on every bench. It doesn't really take much longer. We ride the escalator if she wants to, check out the animals at the pet store, or stop at the fountain for a drink of water.

"I think the key to happy shopping is not to ask too much of the child," says John. "If your kid can't sit in the stroller for a long time, then you have to work harder to make shopping tolerable. Either that, or find a way to leave her at home. You have to know what your child can handle, and respect that."

Eating out

Okay, let's be realistic from the start: if what you want is a leisurely, quiet, romantic meal in a fine dining establishment, you'd best get a babysitter and leave your toddler at home. But you already know that.

Does this mean that toddlers and restaurants don't mix? Not at all. Eating out with your child can be fun, if you do a little planning ahead—starting with the right place at the right time. Some tips from families who learned the hard way:

Think fast, but not too fast. Choose a restaurant with quick service, but preferably one step up from a fast-food chain where you will have to stand in line and carry your own food, while trying to keep some grip on your toddler's whereabouts. Chains like Swiss Chalet and Red Lobster offer food which appeals to both big and little people, welcome families, and have enough bustle and noise that a toddler's high jinks are unlikely to bother anyone. Many have popular features like children's menus and little complimentary toys, but it's the attitude of the staff that is the critical factor. If you have a local diner, you may be pleasantly surprised at how accommodating they are, too.

Go early. Leave lots of time, and avoid "meltdown" hunger. If your toddler is used to eating at six, plan to hit the restaurant by about 5:30 (or feed him at six, and then go out later and let him have a "bedtime snack"). Remember that you'll get faster service if you beat the dinner rush.

Buckle up. Use a high chair rather than a booster, for as long as your toddler will put up with it. Or choose a booth and put the booster chair on the bench between you and the wall, where it is less likely to be accidentally tipped over.

Don't just sit there... Try to minimize the time that your child is expected to sit still. Go for a "walk" before the food arrives, or check out the washroom between courses. Myrtle Fletcher's daughter, Megan, loves going to the salad bar, so they make lots of trips, getting just a small amount of food each time. You can also bring a few little books and toys for those long waits.

Pack a snack. Yes, the whole point of a restaurant is to eat *their* food. But if the service is slow, or he decides restaurant spaghetti is "yucky" that breadstick or container of yogurt might just save the evening. Or look for a restaurant that offers something to eat "while you wait." Myrtle and Megan always enjoy the bowl of nacho chips and cheese sauce that a local Mexican restaurant provides.

Pack everything else, too. Spontaneity is great, but a dirty diaper with no replacement isn't. Also bring your own bib, a washcloth, and a change of clothes, and maybe a spout cup. It's no fun sitting for an hour with orange juice soaking into your tummy!

Order carefully. This is probably not the time to ask your toddler to try some new exotic food; look for something he's eaten before and loves. At this age, many parents just order for themselves and share. (In that case, you don't get to eat new and exotic foods, either.)

And if, despite your good planning, everything falls apart, including everybody's good humour? It might be a good time to head outside for some fresh air, or find some other diversion (if they hand out balloons, for example, at the end of the meal, maybe you could have yours *now*). But if he's clearly finished eating, and you're not, most restaurants will pack up the leftovers for you to take home. Better luck next time!

Going to the doctor

Times change. My easygoing second baby, who charmed everyone in the doctor's office with his trusting smile, was 18 months old...and he was having none of this. He glared defiantly at the nurse who tried to weigh him, and who eventually had to resort to weighing us both together and subtracting my weight. He struggled mightily against taking his shirt off—he who at home was a budding nudist! The crinkle of the paper on the examining table panicked him, and the ear examination provoked outraged howls. And this *before* the needle!

Jesse hadn't had any traumatic medical experience. So why the change in attitude?

Dr. Judith Armstrong, a family physician and mother of three, confirms that one to two is "a difficult age" for doctor's visits. "I'm constantly reassuring parents, 'Don't worry, it gets better!'" she says.

By toddlerhood, babies have grown into very aware individuals, with a healthy suspicion of strangers and a strong sense of their own body. And, Dr. Armstrong adds, it's a year when they get a lot of injections, which they may well remember from visit to visit. So all this resistance is understandable.

Is there anything parents—and doctors—can do to help our toddlers weather these routine check-ups?

Dr. Armstrong uses several strategies to make her check-ups as easy as possible on a child: "First, I try to make the examining room friendly. I have a mobile and other inviting decorations. I always make a point of talking to the child—preferably down at his eye level. I explain what I'm going to do, but I also just make 'small talk'—about his clothes, or how he got here. I like to keep the child on the parent's lap. It's more reassuring than sitting alone on the table."

Dr. Armstrong says she'll take the extra time to help a child get familiar with a procedure: "I'll let him look in my ears first, or I'll look in the parent's ears; I let him hold the stethoscope and see what it is."

Mother of four Kathy Hoehn is a veteran doctor visitor. She always tells her toddlers beforehand that they're going to the doctor's, and talks about what the doctor will check. She stays close to her kids during the exam, holding them on her lap when possible and otherwise touching them and keeping eye contact. "I also try to keep the circumstances pleasant," she explains, "leaving enough time to get ready so that I don't have to grab the kids and rush them out the door, and bringing a small treat for afterwards." Kathy has one more suggestion: "Don't overdress them! Easy-on, easy-off outfits save all kinds of trouble."

Dr. Armstrong has observed that in some instances parents may unwittingly make things worse: "It upsets me when a parent comes in and says, 'My daughter doesn't like doctors. She's just like me!' Children will pick up parents' fears at a very young age." Dr. Armstrong feels it's

---

PLAYING DOCTOR

A good toy doctor's kit is a worthwhile investment at this age, both in terms of play value and to help toddlers become more comfortable at the *real* doctor's. As long as the various "instruments" are sturdy, a basic, inexpensive kit is fine. You might, however, want to purchase a good-quality toy stethoscope, available in better toy and science stores. It will cost about $10, but you can actually hear a heartbeat through it if you position it carefully! After your child's next check-up, your doctor will probably be glad to contribute a real tongue-depressor and the (needle-less) syringe from his immunization.

"Playing doctor" will mostly consist of taking turns giving each other check-ups and treating various ills. As the patient, you will probably find that whether you complain of a runny nose or a sliver in your foot, your child's treatment of choice will be a needle—or maybe lots of needles, in lots of creative places! He's trying to gain some mastery over this frightening aspect of medical care, and have fun lording it over you at the same time. He's the doctor, so roll up your sleeve (or whatever)—but remember what you're modelling. Give a *little* "ouch" each time; don't overdramatize. And when you're the doctor, stick to a more realistic (and reassuring) scenario.

a mistake, too, for well-meaning parents to try to reassure children by telling them that injections won't hurt. "If you say it won't hurt and it does, they won't trust you. I think it's better to be honest, to say, 'You're going to have a needle now. It will hurt, but just for a minute.'"

When a child *has* developed a painful association with the doctor—perhaps after a bout of ear infections or an accident needing stitches—Dr. Armstrong sometimes suggests that parents bring the child just for a visit and quick check, with no unpleasant procedures. This helps the child with a process that happens naturally with most kids: "Around two they start to get more comfortable. They can express themselves, they're more self-confident. . . and there are no more needles for a while!"

A TODDLER-FRIENDLY HOLIDAY:
TIPS FOR A SAFE AND HAPPY SEASON

KIDS BRING A WHOLE NEW MEANING to holidays and family get-togethers. Seen through our baby's wide eyes, the Christmas tree looks taller and more spectacular, the Chanukah candles more mysterious, the extended family more precious. It's a wonderful way to rediscover the power of our traditional festivals.

But parents of busy toddlers need to be aware of the pitfalls of the season, as well. While we often say, "Christmas is for children," for toddlers the holiday season may be a time of stress and confusion. Too young to understand the event that is being anticipated, they sometimes feel ignored by adults who are busy with shopping and parties, or overwhelmed by holiday visitors and excitement. Many parents, though, have found ways to create toddler-friendly holidays that meet their little ones' needs.

Marcia Cudmore, for example, found it important to scale down their Christmas Day "agenda": "Before we had children, we would visit one set of parents on Christmas morning, then drive for a couple of hours to visit the other set for Christmas evening. But when Bethany turned one, we realized it was just too much travelling. So we decided to have Christmas morning at home as a family, and then visit one set of grandparents later Christmas Day. We visit the other grandparents at New Year's and we alternate each year."

Brian Nichols, head of the Early Childhood Education program at Sir Sandford Fleming College, in Peterborough, Ontario, confirms that a hectic visiting pace can be tough on a toddler. "Toddlers visiting a new place need some consistency," he suggests. "Bring along blankets, stuffed toys, favourite foods, things that will comfort them. They'll usually want to stick close to Mom and Dad—which can be difficult for doting relatives, but you should respect that need for security."

SAFE HOLIDAY VISITING

"Holiday visits are prime situations for accidents," cautions Sandra Clarke, executive director of the Advanced Coronary Treatment Foundation and co-author of the Heartsaver Baby course. Think about it. You're in a house that's not babyproofed, but that is full of people, presents and holiday paraphernalia. The adults are extremely busy, not to mention distracted as they catch up on the year's news. And where's little Emily got to . . . ? Clarke offers three basic strategies to keep your visit safe:

- Know who to call in an emergency. "Not all cities have a 911 number," she cautions. Write down all emergency numbers, including the poison control centre, and post them by the phone.
- Babyproof as much as possible. It's not reasonable to completely rearrange your mother-in-law's house for a two-day visit. But you can tactfully ask to take care of the most obvious hazards—move handbags, medications and precious breakables out of reach; lock the door to the basement; gather up empty glasses and beer bottles. And can you bring along your own cupboard locks and baby gates? A car seat for outings and a safe place to sleep are essential.
- Make sure someone is "on duty" with your child at all times. "You'd think with more adults around, your baby would be better supervised," says Clarke. "In fact the reverse is often true." Parents may relax, thinking that "someone else" is keeping an eye on their child, while all the someone elses are thinking the same thing. (I once found my one-year-old in the midst of five adults, happily snacking from a bowl of cat food. No one had even noticed!) If you need a break, specifically delegate someone to take over.

Debby Varendi says Christmas was more successful for her son, Andrew, when the relatives came to visit him. "I just invited everyone to come to our place instead of going to Mom's. Andrew was much more relaxed, and so was I because I didn't have to worry about things not being babyproofed like I do at my parents'. And when he got tired, he could go to sleep in his own room that he was used to."

Whether you celebrate in your own home or across the country, chances are your child's normal routines will go out the window. Some toddlers are so adaptable and easygoing that it's no problem at all. Other children will need your help in coping with all the changes. Is Arden too wound up to nap? Maybe you can spirit her off to a bedroom for a quiet cuddle and some stories, or take her on a drive so that she can relax in her car seat. Is dinner going to be late? Think about what will work best for your child. Your childless cousins may think it's weird when you feed Terry leftover spaghetti an hour before dinner, but then they haven't seen what happens when he's exhausted and starving at the

---

TODDLERS AND HALLOWEEN: A LOVE–HATE RELATIONSHIP

Older children love it. Toddlers . . . Well, toddlers aren't so sure. Seen through a toddler's eyes, Halloween can be downright terrifying. Heck, a *clown* can be terrifying, if you don't know it's supposed to look funny. Halloween is full of grotesque-looking creatures drifting down a dark street—or worse, coming right into your house. No wonder many toddlers find it daunting!

Can you help? Sure. First, tell your toddler about Halloween and what it is in advance. Play dress-up, experiment together with face-paint, so she can understand in a concrete way the difference between costumes and "real." Look at the masks in a department store, and laugh about how "ugly" or "weird" (rather than "scary") they look. Stress that all the trick-or-treaters will be just kids, dressed up.

On the night itself, let your toddler set the pace by inviting, but not pushing. Does she want to dress up? Would she like to come to the door and see the great costumes the kids are wearing? Would she like to hand out some of the treats?

Finally, does she want to go trick-or-treating herself? Most toddlers are happy to go to a few familiar houses; not many are up for a long jaunt (unless they have an older sibling to keep up with—then, look out!) And you'll probably want to skip the really "creepy" houses, the ones with cobwebs, scream tapes, and witches, that are so popular with the big kids.

same time! He may be happier, and better company too, if all he has to do for Christmas dinner is sit on your lap in his PJs and cuddle.

Toddlers, fortunately, are not quite old enough to really be swayed by toy advertising or to demand long lists of gifts. But they can be overwhelmed by the number of presents they receive from doting relatives.

Marcia says: "Gifts can really get out of hand. And toddlers just can't understand the expectation that they wait until Christmas morning to open all those tempting presents under the tree. So we keep the presents hidden until Bethany goes to bed on Christmas Eve." She adds that she follows the same policy of not tempting with decorations. They start halfway up the tree, out of reach of little hands, which are drawn to them like magnets.

Some parents spread out the gifts, instead of saving everything for Christmas morning. "If people visit with presents for Andrew, I let him open them right away, while the people are there," says Debby, adding that it's nicer for the gift-givers, too, when they can see Andrew's pleased reaction.

Marcia feels strongly that parents of toddlers shouldn't try to do too much during the holidays: "There is so much pressure to have elaborate meals, perfectly wrapped presents, elegant parties. The effort of trying to have a perfect holiday can end up making everyone miserable." Think, instead, about what's really important. If you keep your child's needs in mind and focus on just having a nice time together, you'll probably find that child-friendly is much more fun than perfect—even for grown-ups.

Toddler Pleasures:
The Joy of Play

CHILDREN OF ALL AGES PLAY, but in these two years, the complexity
and quality of your child's play changes more dramatically than at
any other time. From the simple exploration he's enjoyed since babyhood, your child will begin to add new elements. He will imitate you,
his brother or the dog. He will sing and dance to music, become
absorbed in a story, deliberately choose the blue marker rather than
grabbing one at random. And as his language, cognitive and imaginative skills all start to blossom, you will see the emergence of true

8 7

"pretend play" (and no doubt find yourself, from time to time, cast in the role of a horsey or TV character). With his new imaginative ability, his play becomes more emotive, and he may develop a deep affection for his stuffed bear or the worm he finds in the garden, and weep with real grief if his "playmate" dries up in the sun and dies.

Your child doesn't make a distinction between play and "real life." Helping you make real cookies, or making Play-Doh cookies—it's all play if it's fun, and absorbing, and what he wants to do. He will benefit in different ways from playing alone, from playing with you, and (especially as he nears three) from playing with other children, just as he benefits from access to a variety of play materials and activities—but he doesn't need a lot of elaborate, expensive toys or programs.

By now, most parents have heard the phrase "play is a child's work." It's well-meaning, and true enough, stressing as it does the value and importance of play to children's learning and development. But it hardly captures the *spirit* of play, the whimsy, the freedom—above all, the sheer pleasure of it. Yes, children at play *are* practising fine-motor control, mastering science concepts, studying adult roles. But the irony is, if you over-focus on the "learning" aspect, you start turning play into something much more structured and limiting. You don't have to build learning into play. You just have to let it happen—and enjoy.

ROLL, CUDDLE, STACK, DUMP:
BEST TODDLER TOYS

OY COLLECTIONS, BY THEIR NATURE, tend to grow in a haphazard and often lopsided way (starting with the zillion stuffed bears your baby probably received within weeks of her birth). But from time to time, it's worth taking stock of your child's toys, as well as her development. What's missing? What is she ready for? The well-rounded toybox needn't be stuffed with expensive items, but it should include materials that engage your child's growing interests and abilities in a variety of different ways.

Toy consultant Julie Creighton cautions us, though, to be attuned to our children's pleasure as much as to a toy's "developmental correctness." "By around age two, children are already developing their own play styles. Some like to be the star of their own show—these are the kids who love dress-up clothes and realistic 'props' to go with them—while others are 'scene setters' who like to direct the action, and who gravitate to miniature playsets where they can move around the people or cars." It's important, says Creighton, to observe your child's play and honour his preferences. And that includes how he uses the toys he has: "Children need the freedom to play and explore in their own way: they don't *have* to stack a stacking toy."

That said, here's Creighton's "quick sketch" of toddlers' play development.

12 to 18 months: Creighton calls this the age of "I can do!" Just-one-year-olds enjoy activities that demonstrate their growing mastery without demanding too much co-ordination: dumping out, filling up, putting together, knocking down. Water toys, stacking toys, buckets full of blocks (or a drawer full of T-shirts) to dump and replace, and big, lightweight balls to toss and chase are fun at this age.

THE TOY LIBRARY
Toy libraries are
starting to spring up
across the country,
especially through
family resource pro-
grams. A real boon to
parents on a budget
and those who prefer
to "try before they
buy," toy libraries
bring novelty and
excitement to any
child's collection. As a
bonus, the people
involved in running
the toy library,
whether paid staff or
volunteers, usually
get to know a lot
about toys and can
suggest good bets for
your baby's age.
Membership fees are
usually nominal and
more than worth it.
Inquire with your
local family service
agencies to see if
there's a toy library
in your community.

18 to 24 months: "These kids are shovers and luggers," says Creighton. "They like to push around a shopping cart or doll buggy, and this is a good time to introduce a good, stable foot-to-floor vehicle—although they are likely to carry it around at first rather than ride it." By the end of this stage, imaginative play begins to blossom. A toy telephone will be played with for months to come: "First it's a manipulative toy. It's fun to turn the dial, or make it squeak. Then you'll see the child 'talking' on the phone. Later still, she'll pretend she's Mommy talking on the phone, or that Grandpa's talking back," says Creighton.

24 to 36 months: Communication skills and imaginative play come to the fore. "Toys are talked about more now," notes Creighton, "and children will stretch out their play longer, creating a little story with their toys." This is the age to introduce basic pretend toys—a tea set for parties with friends and bears, a work-shop, a doctor's kit. Don't overlook the possibilities of "real stuff": a little fry pan, a plastic flipper, and some cereal to "cook" will add appeal to his play stove, while a dustpan and brush will let him really help (ha!) you sweep up. Miniature playscapes offer a different kind of pretend play: a barn with animals, a garage with cars. "By 30 months, if not before, you should start paying attention to your child's own play style and preferences," says Creighton. "Which playset will spark his imagination?"

Creighton notes that some really good toys—like simple puzzles—

have a limited lifespan: "Because toddlers are changing so rapidly, a toy that's perfect today may be grown out of in three months." Luckily, she adds, at this age it's easy to expand the toy collection with interesting household objects: "Empty yogurt containers can be nested into each other, or filled with treasures, or arranged upside down in a row. And a big cardboard box has all kinds of possibilities. Of course," she cautions, "you have to give anything in your cupboard a really good going-over for safety—expecting it to be abused, not handled gently!—before offering it to a toddler."

Other toys introduced during the toddler years will be basics for years to come. Some suggestions:

A good set of wooden blocks or plastic building bricks will grow along with her abilities. They'll be used first for dumping out with a satisfying rumble. Stacks or "roads" of blocks come later, castles and zoo cages later still.

Play-Doh will be squished, poked, and pulled apart with great pleasure as early as 12 months (but watch that it's not eaten!) By two, a set of simple gadgets will extend the play: cookie cutters or moulds, textured objects to make prints, maybe some little plastic animals to stick on a Play-Doh "mountain." Toddlers may find home-made playdough, which can be made a little softer, easier to manage at first than the commercial product.

TOY RESOURCES

The Toy Report is published annually (each October) by the Canadian Toy Testing Council (CTTC). Rating and reporting on hundreds of toys, it's invaluable when it comes to the final selection. Available at bookstores and libraries, or by mail order from the CTTC. Phone or write for an order form: 22 Hamilton Avenue North, Ottawa, Ontario K1Y 1B6; (613) 729-7101.

Your Baby and Child, by Penelope Leach, Alfred A. Knopf, 1989, includes a seven-page chart (from page 354) full of toy and activity suggestions for toddlers.

"Why do they always make little kids' toys all colourful and, well, childish looking? I keep thinking that if I could find a toy that looked real—something silver, with buttons and wires and digital displays—Chelsea might want to play with that instead of our VCR remote."

Art materials. Bring them out as soon as he can refrain from eating them, certainly by age two. Fat crayons are sturdy and easy to grasp. Non-toxic washable markers are easier to use and make exciting bright streaks of colour.

Some of your old clothes—hats, slippers, shirts with the arms cut short—are the perfect start to her dress-up box, which will provide solitary and shared play throughout the preschool years. Or you can splurge on a toy firefighter's hat, a cape or a crown.

Cuddly friends: Not a zillion stuffed animals, but a few soft dolls and bears to hug, scold and talk to.

Finally, don't forget books and music. Babies who enjoy sharing books with Mom and Dad will eventually spend a surprising amount of time alone with their bookshelf. As for music, the Canadian kids' music scene is bursting with talent (Raffi is still a great place to start for the very young), but play him your music too: nobody can twist and shout like a two-year-old!

TODDLERS AND THE TUBE
Is TV an appropriate toddler "toy"? Although most of the literature on television and children focuses on older age groups, most toddlers do watch and enjoy television. But because their ability to "process" words and pictures has not matured and their life experience is so limited (how can they judge what is realistic and what isn't?), they don't understand most television in the way that older children can.

"They really don't understand the difference between fantasy and real-ity, and the fast pace of most programming—the flow of words, music and sound effects, the speed of the pictures—is very difficult for them to make sense of," says Kealy Wilkinson, national director of the Alliance for Children and Television. Some toddlers, admittedly, are mesmerized by this stream of stimulation, "but they're only really getting little bits."

What works for a toddler? Most parents, says Wilkinson, instinctively (and rightly) avoid content that is frightening or violent. Equally impor-tant, though, is to look for a slower pace and predictable story line. "Toddlers are just mastering language, just learning about the world," she says. "They need programs that allow them to keep up." Although the dra-matic sound and colour of commercial cartoons has instant appeal for chil-dren, their very "busyness" makes them hard for under-threes to follow. Wilkinson notes that even *Sesame Street*, deservedly popular though it is, moves too quickly for many toddlers; there's no time to assimilate one "story" before the next is on. The homey, easygoing approach of *Mr. Dressup* or *Big Comfy Couch* is a better fit for most little ones.

If this is your first child, now is the time to start developing family norms around TV viewing. While your baby was oblivious, you may have watched adult shows while nursing or cuddling her to sleep on the couch. Now you need to become aware of what she's being exposed to; after all, the news can be one of the most harrowing programs on the air. If your TV is on as "background" much of the time, you may want to change your habits. Even when the programming is age-appropriate, you need to think about how *much* television you are comfortable with. Heavy television view-ing has clearly been shown to be detrimental to the development of chil-dren's imagination, reading skills and fitness levels. Wilkinson points out that toddlers are "designed" to learn about the world in an intensely tactile and sensual way—even more than older children, they need to move, touch, and manipulate, as well as listen and watch. While no one can tell you just how much TV is okay for your child, media and child development experts agree that, for toddlers, a little goes a long way.

"READ ME A STORY": LEARNING TO LOVE BOOKS

Where is the keeper who keeps at the zoo?
The wolf wants to know, and the kangaroo ...

I WAS ON A TRAIN FROM TORONTO TO Montreal with my 18-month-old son, and *Where Is the Keeper* was wearing a little thin. In fact, I was ready to strangle both the author of this little piece of doggerel, and the well-meaning mom who had passed it on to us. But Riley, who was starting to know the story well enough to fill in some of the rhymes, loved it more passionately than ever. We spent a good part of that five-hour trip reading it over, and over, and over ... Hey, if it keeps a toddler happy and quiet in a moving vehicle, you do it!

Happily, reading to toddlers isn't usually an act of parental endurance—far from it. Many parents count it one of their favourite ways to spend time together.

"What do we get out of reading with Kelly?" asks her mom, Sue Coz. "You name it! Closeness—sitting on my lap or next to me, snuggled with her Bunny. I can see how she's learning the names of objects—now she points them out to me! And it's a chance to share a good laugh together, at the sillier parts of the books."

Parents like Sharon Setterington, mother of two-year-old Cecilia, don't need any convincing of the value of reading with toddlers. "My mother taught me when I was young that 'whenever you have a book, you have a friend,' and I hope to teach that to my daughter as well," she explains.

Educator Paul Kropp, author of *The Reading Solution*, sees lots of educational value to early exposure to books. "Children begin to form concepts of 'the world as a story' by age two," says Kropp. "Reading to them helps their intellectual development, and also sets the stage for literacy by giving them the basic idea of what reading is: that there are stories; that the pictures support the stories; that you turn the pages in a certain order, and so on."

Kropp hastens to add that he is *not* talking about trying to teach toddlers to actually read. "There are no long-term benefits to early reading instruction of any kind," he stresses. Much more important, says Kropp, is the "positive association with books that children develop through enjoying stories with their parents."

Reading to a toddler is different from reading to an older child, though, and parents who expect quiet attentiveness may be in for frustration. "It's quite common for Mom or Dad to be reading away while the kid is crawling under the covers, coming up now and then to check the pictures. That's okay; don't misinterpret wiggling as lack of interest!" says Kropp. Other toddlers interrupt during the story, because they want to talk about the pictures, ask questions, or name what they see. That, too, says Kropp, is a great way to share a book.

The toddler attention span is notoriously short, so "you have to be ready to pick up a book when they are interested," says Kropp. "Early in this age-group, you're more likely to get four or five minutes at a time than one long reading session. A lot of parents have told me they like reading to their toddler during bathtime. It's ideal because the child is already relaxed and sort of contained."

Bringing books into a toddler's life needn't be expensive, says Kropp. "You don't have to buy the big $25 picture book. It's too soon, and you'll just be struggling with the child about keeping it nice. At this age, children need to actively explore their books. Sturdy little board books and inexpensive paperbacks are ideal."

What makes a good book for a toddler? While there are plenty of theoretical guidelines, the best advice is simply: experiment! The idea that babies progress, from "theme" or "object" books (where each page is basically a named illustration that stands alone) to stories, from simple

TODDLER HIT-PARADE

Your toddler is the ultimate authority on what she likes! That said, there are many, many titles that have consistently pleased babies and their parents; your children's librarian or bookseller will have lots of suggestions. To get you started, here are a few of our favourites for toddlers who are ready for a "real"—but not too long—story.

- *Each Peach, Pear, Plum*, by Janet Ahlberg and Allan Ahlberg (Puffin)
- *The Going to Bed Book*, by Sandra Boynton (Boynton Board Books)
- *Good Night, Moon*, by Margaret Wise Brown (HarperCollins)
- *Rosie's Walk*, by Pat Hutchins (Macmillan)
- *The Very Hungry Caterpillar*, by Eric Carle (Philomel)
- The *Zoe* series (*Zoe's Rainy Day; Zoe's Sunny Day; Zoe's Snowy Day; Zoe's Windy Day*), by Barbara Reid (HarperCollins)
- *Toes Are to Tickle*, by Shen Roddie (Tricycle Press)
- Any well-illustrated nursery rhyme book
- Almost any toddler book by Shirley Hughes or Helen Oxenbury

illustrations to more detailed, complex pictures, from very short text to a longer text, is fine as far as it goes. But it doesn't account for individual quirks, and those quirks are all-important. Some children love point-and-name picture books, and will explore them with enthusiasm for years. Others, like my Riley, will quickly dismiss these books and demand that you "read the story!" However your child enjoys books ("short of eating them," quips Kropp) is fine.

Don't feel you must be limited, either, to traditional toddler books. Many's the second or third child who has listened to an older sibling's bedtime stories, and been the richer for it. Young children soak up the language and excitement of good stories, even if they don't fully understand the action. If your toddler has a special interest, check remainder bins in your local bookstore for a lavishly photographed reference book on the topic. (Animals are big in our house, and we've had huge mileage out of a cut-rate animal encyclopedia, now held together with miles of strapping tape, and an old *Dogs in Canada* catalogue.) You can also make a customized toddler book with a small photo album. Fill it with photos of her favourite people and places, or with magazine pictures of familiar objects. It's easy, cheap and renewable!

Finally, when possible, choose a book that *you* will like, too. Because if it's a hit, you're going to be reading it for a long, long time. And while Kropp readily admits that we adults may have trouble dealing with the repetition, he explains that toddlers gain a wonderful sense of comfort and mastery from rereading a well-known book. "Of course young children also enjoy new and different books," he writes in *The Reading Solution,* "but it is in repeated reading of favourite books that real gains are made in understanding stories and language."

Sharon Setterington observes how deeply Cecilia has absorbed her favourite stories: "Cecilia now enjoys sitting in a chair and looking through her books by herself," observes Sharon. "It's really cute to watch; she turns each page (never missing one) and will talk out loud to her dolly about what is happening. It's amazing how much of the story she can pass on to her doll without help."

For Cecilia, books are already familiar friends. It's a relationship that can only get better.

BUT IS IT ART?: TODDLER CRAFTS THAT WORK

THE MINUTE SHE GETS IN THE DOOR of the parent–child drop-in centre, Alannah makes a beeline for the painting easel. She waits impatiently, arms in the air, for her mom to catch up and help her into the big apron that protects her clothing. Alannah, at 22 months, already knows the ropes—she's visited this giant playroom many times.

Now is her big moment. She hovers over the row of paint pots, considering. A bright red streak. A yellow streak, with a trailing drip that happens all by itself. A couple of scrubby green dots. And she's out of there, moving on to the rocking horse. Before she goes home, Alannah will make an equally brief pit-stop at the pasting table, and spend quite a long time poking, pulling and squishing the yellow, peppermint-scented Play-Doh. As they are getting ready to head home, Alannah's mom collects her nearly dry painting. "It's lovely, Alannah. What is it?" she asks innocently. Alannah fixes her mother with a blank, *I-have-no-idea-what-you're-talking-about* stare.

One day, Alannah will, indeed, set out to draw or paint a recognizable figure. But that day is still far away. Right now, her "arts and crafts" are "really discovery/sensory activities," explains Sue Martin, an early childhood education professor at Centennial College in Toronto. Toddlers are into process, not product. In their quest to discover what the world is all about, they are, perhaps, the ultimate experimenters. And so, when they approach art materials, their goal is not so much to make anything in particular, but rather to explore more basic issues: What is this stuff? What does it do? What can I do with it? What happens if I...?

The results may not look much like an adult's concept of art, especially if the question for the day is: "What happens if I cover everything

9 8

with black and scrub it in hard?" But Martin assures us that toddlers still get many benefits from simple craft activities.

"Access to art materials helps to develop a toddler's concentration and basic fine motor skills: the ability to grasp, hold and manipulate small objects. It allows them to, literally, get a handle on the world. As they get a little older, they start to become more intentional about what they're doing—I want to do it *this* way—and this is a chance for them to set their own goals and gain a sense of mastery." Martin points out that since art activities usually require close adult supervision, the resulting interaction also gives lots of opportunities to develop language skills.

What kinds of activities and materials are best for toddlers? "Toddlers need to experience success," notes Martin, "so it's important that the materials not be beyond their abilities." The watercolour trays with solid paint discs, for example, and many gluing activities require too much co-ordination for a toddler.

"The one thing you do have to be very careful of is to avoid any potentially toxic ingredients," cautions Martin, "since even toddlers who don't actually try to eat the supplies will probably get the stuff on their hands and eventually into their mouths."

Some tips for fun toddler art:

Scribbling and painting: The regular skinny crayons prove pretty fragile under a toddler's clenched fist—you'll save money and frustration by investing in the sturdier fat crayons. Fat washable markers are easier still, allowing your toddler to focus on the lovely streaks of colour he's making rather than pressing hard enough to make a mark.

Painting is definitely a messy activity, but it's more "sensory" and satisfying than scribbling. Finger-paints are a natural first painting experience. Commercial finger-paint is available, but you can also make your own or (if you don't have a problem with mixing food and play) use edible products like pudding or coloured yogurt. Rather than going through sheaves of expensive finger-paint paper, your child can finger-paint on

SENSORAMA
Sue Martin reminds us to "think about all five senses, not just the visual," when giving our toddlers creative experiences. Through visual art materials, children explore colour, shape and light. But smell, texture, taste and sounds are also important. We don't usually think of smelling spices, listening to the sound of a brush rubbed against different objects, or crawling over a bunch of different surfaces taped to a floor as art activities—yet a keen sensory awareness contributes to all the arts.

her high-chair tray or on a cookie sheet. When she's done, lay a piece of ordinary paper over the paint and—*ta-da!*—instant abstract print.

For "real" painting, liquid tempera paint is probably best. It is less expensive to buy powder and mix it, but the premixed squirt bottles are less trouble and a better texture. Whatever you're using, you might want to thicken it with a little flour or cornstarch to minimize drips. (Only thicken small amounts at a time, as it won't keep this way.) Start with only one or two colours, each with its own brush. Karen Miller, author of *Things to Do with Toddlers and Twos* (Telshare Publishing, 1984), suggests that small, six-inch-long trim brushes from a hardware store are easier for little ones to manage than the standard long easel brushes.

What about paper? Whatever is at hand will be fine. Toddlers will happily paint on newspapers, brown paper bags, or the back of your junk mail. Parents of real painting fiends might want to buy a roll of white paper or newsprint that can be cut to length (try school supply stores, IKEA, or your local newspaper). Here's a paperless painting idea, from Martin: pour oil and a few squirts of food colouring (for better colour, mix it in a little milk first) into a Ziploc bag. Seal it *securely*, and let your child make changing colour patterns by poking and gooshing the bag.

Play-Doh: As soothing as kneading bread, Play-Doh is an undemanding medium with myriad possibilities. Let your toddler start by simply poking, squishing, and tearing off hunks of the stuff. Later, you can give her

---

HOME-MADE PLAYDOUGH

Everyone has a favourite recipe. Here's one that's long-lasting and safe if your little one sneaks a taste:

4 cups	flour
2 cups	salt
4 tablespoons	cream of tartar
4 cups	water (add food colour as desired)
2 tablespoons	oil

Mix ingredients in a pot. Stir over medium heat until it stiffens up. Let cool and knead.

---

things to poke and print with—her baby fork, a blunt butter knife, a dinosaur to make footprints. As her vocabulary and imagination grow, the Play-Doh will start to remind her of things, and you'll soon find yourself adding birthday-cake candles, little play figures to live in the "cave," or a pizza wheel. A parent's participation in this pretend play (with your child as leader and you in the supporting role) can enrich it enormously and be great fun for both of you.

Homemade playdough tends to be a little softer than the commercial product, so it's easier for toddlers to handle (though not as good for actual modelling). For a real sensory treat, give her freshly made playdough while it's still warm.

"As toddlers, one of my children would go to a painting easel and systematically make a vertical line of each colour, [whereas] the other scrubbed and dotted and blobbed. And you know, to this day my first child has a very orderly, mathematical mind, while the second is more free-wheeling."

Glue/pasting: Gluing with toddlers can be a great success or a sticky nightmare. Your tactful help is probably required, if only to wield the washcloth when your gummed-up toddler gets frustrated that every-thing wants to stick to *him* rather than the paper.

For simple paper sticking, a home-made flour-and-water paste is eas-ier for a toddler to work with than standard white craft glue; it's "for-giving" because it's not sticky until it dries. You can put a little in a container with a paint-brush, and your child can either gob it all over the page and then put the collage items wherever he wants, or brush the paste directly on the bigger pieces.

Commercial glue *is* fun to dribble from a squeeze bottle in trails. Your toddler can then sprinkle sand, cornmeal, etc., over the page. Let it dry, pour off the loose sprinkles, and show him the pattern he's made.

For any kind of pasting, a heavy-duty backing like cardboard or con-struction paper is a good idea.

One final point. When we are urged to allow our toddlers to "do their own thing" with art materials, we may feel we are being told *never* to do more structured projects with them. "But Adrian loved the train we made together out of cardboard boxes," you might think, or "Jenny was so pleased with the collage we made with leaves and flowers we col-lected on our walk. What's wrong with helping her make something pretty?" It's not wrong. Toddlers can get real satisfaction out of these joint projects—but do be aware that this is an altogether different activ-ity. You could think of it this way: when you sit down to make a collage to give to Grandma, it's like making cookies together. You are the leader and she is the helper. But when *she* is gloriously in the driver's seat, deciding for herself what to do with that big, blank paper, she can fol-low her own star. And isn't that what children's play—and the greatest art—are both about?

THOSE WIDE OPEN SPACES: THE BENEFITS OF OUTDOOR PLAY

AUL EAGLES, OUTDOOR EDUCATION professor at University of Waterloo, remembers a camping trip with a family that included a toddler. The parents were quite concerned that their child not get dirty while playing outside—so much so that they had a bucket of water at the entrance to the tent, where the little boy was required to wash off his toys before bringing them inside. Any dirt or mud on his hands or legs was immediately washed off; if his clothes got messy, he had to change them.

Eagles says, "I guess it goes without saying that the family didn't enjoy camping very much. Getting dirty is an expected part of outdoor play for small children."

But Eagles feels strongly that any dirt and mess involved are well worth it when balanced against all the benefits of outdoor play. Once the warm weather has settled in, parents and toddlers are both usually eager to get outside. Some families have large backyards, while others take advantage of neighbourhood playgrounds. Eagles reminds parents that it is also important for children to have the experience of playing in a natural environment.

The current trend, he points out, is for an increasing percentage of families to live in ever-growing cities. That means rural and wild landscapes are simply not part of our everyday lives. Even the green spaces and parks in our neighbourhoods tend to be carefully manicured lawns dotted with metal frames for swings and slides. That doesn't meet the need that Eagles sees for contact with nature.

"There are both physical and psychological benefits to being in contact with the natural world," Eagles explains. "It shows children the expansiveness of nature, the existence of a big world beyond walls, cars and parking lots. And small children love nature—I've never known one that didn't."

THE WALK, TODDLER-STYLE

If you actually need to get somewhere, walking with a toddler can be an exercise in frustration. But as an *activity*, it can hardly be beat. The secret? Think "explore," not "travel."

In every season, a short walk either on your own street or in a natural setting will unearth untold wonders. Smell that spring rain smell. Point out the going-to-seed dandelions and let her blow them away. Find the most beautiful fall leaf ever. Check out what the telephone repair crew is up to. Bring a bag to collect the "treasures" she finds.

In really terrible weather, go for an "explore" inside. Check out the live trout or lobsters at the grocery store, or take the top off your toilet tank and show her how it works.

Remember, just about everything in the world is new to your child. Her curiosity and capacity for discovery are boundless. And if your "walk" only gets as far as the fascinating puddle in your driveway, that's just fine. You've still reached your destination.

For most families, visits to a natural setting can be done only on weekends or holidays and won't satisfy the average toddler's urge to play outside. Fortunately, a wide range of outdoor toys are now available that foster active outdoor play in your own backyard or neighbourhood park.

In a review of these toys, the Canadian Toy Testing Council (CTTC) writes in its annual publication, *The Toy Report*: "Sliding and splashing, climbing and jumping, balancing and swinging—these sets encourage children to do what they do best!...Testing families were almost unanimous in saying how much their children had enjoyed the physical aspects of play with these toys." The report adds that imaginative play also gets a workout with these toys, as the climbing frame becomes a store, a hospital, a pirate ship, a haunted house.

For toddlers, plastic play structures that incorporate features of both a playhouse and climbing frame (often with a small slide, as well) are safest and easiest to manage. Many can be moved indoors (if you have the space in a basement or family room) to extend their play value. Larger climbing structures and traditional swing sets will keep their appeal for many years but require very close supervision when young children are involved. This rule is even more crucial when visiting a neighbourhood or school play-ground, where the equipment is generally designed for older children and can be hazardous for toddlers.

"I don't think a bucket of toads is on any list of recommended toys for toddlers! But some older children brought over a bunch of toads they had caught, and Carling was completely fascinated. There's just something about living nature that no toy can compete with."

As the CTTC points out, all of these toys are expensive, and the more elaborate climbing frames can easily cost several hundred dollars. Their recommendation—buy when your child is at the youngest end of the recommended age range, so that you will get the maximum use of the item.

But don't feel your toddler will be deprived without an expensive climber. At this age, a modest array of basic toys will provide plenty of play opportunities. A ride-on toy or wagon will get good use; so will bouncy balls, sidewalk chalk, or a blanket draped over your picnic table!

Sand and water are the two "basic" play materials for children of all ages. Even a small plastic sandbox on an apartment balcony will provide many hours of enjoyment. On days when you can stand a little mess, provide water to pour and mix into the sand (damp sand is less likely to fly into your child's hair and eyes, anyway). Keep your sandbox covered when not in use to discourage cats from using it as a litter box.

Even the smallest backyard wading pool requires constant supervision, but most parents agree there's nothing better on a hot afternoon. Some toddlers have even more fun just playing with the dribbling hose.

Whether you are heading to a provincial park or your own backyard for outdoor play, Paul Eagles adds one more warning: remember to protect your child from the sun. "Children, especially light-skinned children, have sensitive skin and we sometimes forget how easily they burn

WINTER . . . FUN?

For older kids, winter brings a whole new set of outdoor pleasures: skating, sledding, snowmen . . . But when a toddler is immobilized in a heavy snowsuit and boots, unable to grasp anything in her stiff, slippery mitts, literally up to her thighs in snow, her play opportunities are limited. Here's how creative Canadian parents have managed to enjoy the Great Canadian Winter with their little ones:

- Shovel out a circular play area in your yard or park, piling up the snow in sloping "walls" all around. The walls provide a windbreak, and the inside becomes a cosy little "house" where your toddler can actually walk. Kick around a beach ball, share a snack, clamber up and slide down the walls . . .
- Try "snow painting" with a spray bottle of food colouring and water, or poster paints and big brushes.
- Your toddler can toboggan on a gentle slope if you sit behind her to steer and support.
- Your umbrella stroller won't be much use on slushy sidewalks, but it's great on a skating rink. Push your toddler along as you skate: a workout for you, an exhilarating ride for him.
- Increase your mobility with a backpack, baby sled, or large-wheeled jogging stroller.
- Invest in good outdoor wear. It may be outgrown quickly, but you can either resell it or save it for the next baby. Waterproof, elbow-length mitts, snowpants with elasticized cuffs, and really warm boots can make the difference between comfort and misery.
- At least once, take your baby out on a calm, snowy winter night. Lie down in a snowbank together, and admire the uncannily bright sky, the swirls around the streetlights, and the snowflakes sprinkling around you. It really is amazing.

in the sun. Avoid direct sun in the middle of the day, have your children wear hats, and use a good sunscreen whenever they're outside."

A SONG AND A TICKLE: FINGERPLAY FUN

Round and round the garden
Goes the teddy bear
One step, two steps
TICKLE you under there!

YOUR CHILD'S GIGGLES, AS YOU WALK your fingers around his palm and up his arm, are reason enough to have a fingerplay or two up your sleeve. But did you know that those silly verses are also a valuable educational activity?

Professor Betty Flint of the Parent–Infant Centre in the University of Toronto's Institute of Child Study explains that songs, nursery rhymes and fingerplays are very valuable for all young children learning about language. "Through songs and nursery rhymes, the young child learns the rhythm and the sounds of the language of his culture," she says. "He may not understand all of them, but the pathways are being established in his brain, and this is the basis for language."

Your toddler, of course, isn't thinking about learning language skills. To her, it's the close, warm interaction and the fun she is having while you sing the songs and help her imitate the actions that matter. She's getting the message that she's loved and that you enjoy playing with her.

"There is an entire therapy program, for parents who are having trouble relating to their babies, that is based on songs, nursery rhymes and storytelling," says Flint. "The therapist encourages the parents to sing songs and tell the child rhymes and stories—if they're feeling awkward about talking to the child, these provide a ready-made form of communication. And most parents soon learn to enjoy themselves."

Most of the traditional songs for children are sung with a lot of expression that emphasizes and reveals the meaning to the child. The

"BUT I DON'T KNOW ANY SONGS!"

For parents who have forgotten the songs and rhymes of their own childhood, a visit to any toy store, children's bookstore, or video rental outlet will uncover an overwhelming number of tapes, videos and books that will bring back all the old songs and teach you dozens of new ones. You might look for:

- *Baby Games*, by Elaine Martin, Stoddart Press, 1988
- *Round and Round the Garden*, by Sara Williams, Oxford University Press, 1983.

Of the many children's musicians, Sharon, Lois and Bram are particularly fond of songs that include actions. Their pace is a little too brisk for most toddlers, but *you* can borrow a video from the library, learn a song or two, and slow it down.

actions do the same thing. Many parents, for example, will know "The Wheels on the Bus," a popular song with an endless number of verses in which the child imitates the swish-swish of the windshield wipers, the bumping up and down of passengers, the crying of the babies, and any creative additions the singers can think up. (Our buses often included alligators going snap-snap-snap and other exotic passengers.) This song is the most fun when the driver (who tells the passengers to "Move on back!") is sung with a very gruff voice, the crying babies are loud and miserable, and the soothing parents are tender and almost whispering.

Explains Flint: "The exaggeration in the actions, voices and expressions adds impact and excitement, and helps the child become involved in the song. There is a great range of emotions expressed in children's songs as well, from humour to drama ('Humpty Dumpty had a great fall!') to the comforting lullabies."

Flint points out that traditional rhymes also teach the child something of the history of her culture. They are filled with the elements of folklore and fairy tale that provide a background to adult literary traditions. As well, these rhymes and songs carry the cadence and inflections of the child's language, which are important elements of communication.

The rhyming in both nursery rhymes and songs help children learn language by reinforcing memory. Daddy recites: "Humpty Dumpty sat on a *wall*, Humpty Dumpty had a great *fall*," and his emphasis draws his daughter's attention to the similarities and differences between the two words. The rhyme will help her remember the phrases today, and will help her again in years to come when she begins reading and discovers that rhyming words are often written the same way as well.

Brenda Bunting experienced an especially moving example of the magic of action songs and rhymes.

Because her daughter, Zoe, has cerebral palsy, it was difficult at first to tell how much she understood when spoken to. When her arm moved slightly as someone said "Bye-bye," Brenda could never be sure if it was a real attempt to wave or a meaningless twitch.

Then, Brenda remembers, at the suggestion of Zoe's therapist, "I started singing all the traditional songs to her. With one, I touched the different parts of her body as they were named in the song, and finishing up by tickling her." Brenda hadn't repeated the song very many times before she could see Zoe beginning to anticipate what was coming next—she raised her hand to have the palm stroked, and turned her head from one side to the other so each ear could be touched. And as the tickling part approached, she started to giggle. "That was a wonderful moment for me," says Brenda. "I could see not only that she understood it, but that she was enjoying it. It was very exciting for both of us."

Canadian parents are fortunate to have access to a wide range of songs, both traditional and new, that can be shared with their children. (If you want actions, and the song doesn't have any, feel free to make them up.)

"Singing these action songs together is rewarding for both parents and their toddlers," Flint says. "Singing has gone out of our culture—we don't sing much ourselves, we listen to other people singing for us. But once we

ONE TO GET YOU STARTED
This traditional rhyme requires no singing, and is enjoyed by infants and toddlers alike.

Head of hair	**(stroke the child's hair)**
Forehead bare	**(run a finger along his forehead)**
Eye winker, Tom tinker	**(touch under each eye, in turn)**
Nose dropper	**(touch his nose)**
Mouth eater	**(touch his mouth)**
Chin chopper, chin chopper,	
CHIN CHOPPER!	**(depending on your child's temperament, tickle or kiss gently or uproariously under the chin)**

start singing with our children, we find out we really enjoy it."

And toddlers are a very accepting audience—your baby will never complain about a few wrong notes or the sections where you have to hum because you've forgotten some of the words. She'll think you're the best show in town—because for her, you are!

SIDE BY SIDE: THE BEGINNING OF SOCIAL PLAY

I'm out on the sidewalk with 19-month-old Aaron, where we meet our next-door neighbour and her two young charges: Lauren (16 months) and Connor (20 months). As the mothers chat, the kiddies stare solemnly at each other. Finally Connor helps himself to one of the plastic shopping carts on our lawn, and begins pushing it along the sidewalk. Lauren and Aaron promptly make a beeline for the second cart, and a heated tug-of-war ensues until I bring out another push toy. Soon all three toddlers are intently bustling up and down the walk with their carts, utterly absorbed. By and large, they copy each other's play without directly interacting. Yet it's clear that part of the fun of the game lies in doing it in company with the others.

his is "parallel play," the classic social play of toddlerhood. Not quite playing "with" each other, but nevertheless aware of each other's presence, toddlers often enjoy playing side by side, even though by adult standards they may seem indifferent to each other.

"We often place too much emphasis on a child becoming sociable at an early age," says Sue Martin, a professor at Toronto's Centennial College who specializes in infant and toddler development. She cautions that it's not realistic to expect toddlers to manage the complex skills (like sharing, taking turns or negotiating the "rules" of a game) that characterize more mature interactive play: "The child is still only able to function from his own perspective. He is still developing his own sense of self; he can't empathize with the other child's point of view or reason about how to solve a conflict." To make matters even more difficult, most toddlers have limited language skills, and may well find each other quite unintelligible.

Does this mean we shouldn't bother exposing our toddlers to other little "friends"? Not at all. There's a surprising richness to some parallel play, as T. Berry Brazelton has observed. In his book *Touchpoints* (Addison-Wesley, 1992), he writes: "The most wonderful thing I know of is to watch two children of this age playing in close proximity...They never seem to look at each other. Yet they...seem to absorb play patterns through peripheral vision. Whole sequences of toy play and of communication are repeated. Think of the amount and quality of learning that are contained in such close imitation."

This kind of learning can only take place, though, if a child is comfortable enough to become absorbed in her play. It's important to be sensitive to her individual temperament. Some toddlers will breeze into a playground, sashay up to the sandbox and squeeze right in, glorying in the crowd. Others find a group of unknown children intimidating, and will play more happily with just one or two familiar friends, or after a lengthy "warm-up" period on Mom's lap.

Since toddlers really can't solve their own conflicts at this age (their negotiating skills being generally limited to clutching, screaming and a good hard shove), prevention is the best policy. Plenty of equipment for everyone (yes, *three* push toys!) and alert adults who can head trouble off at the pass will help.

While the researchers who first categorized children's play some 50 years ago believed that toddlers were essentially limited to parallel play until at least age three and a half, the first steps towards interactive play can often be observed much earlier:

Another day. Aaron and Lauren are in the sandbox together. Classic parallel play again: each has a shovel, each is digging away, but they are not playing with each other. Or are they? As I watch, Aaron reaches over and pours a shovelful of sand into Lauren's

GOOD PARALLEL PLAY ACTIVITIES FOR TODDLERS

It's playgroup day. You're expecting four toddlers, and no, you can't supply four ride-on toys. Knowing that toddlers aren't so great at taking turns, what can you offer them that's easy to share? How about:

- Play-Doh: four chairs, four hunks of dough and a couple of gadgets each
- Group art: tape down a big sheet of newsprint or brown paper, and pass around markers or crayons
- Dress-up clothes. No need for fancy costumes at this age. An array of old clothes, hats and scarves—in front of a nice big mirror—will do fine.
- A big bin of Duplo or wooden blocks
- In warm weather, water or sand play (with a good assortment of shovels, pails, pouring things and bath toys)
- A well-timed snack. Think little, easily managed finger foods.

If the toys are spread out a little, the children are more likely to spread out, too, and less likely to all glom onto the same thing at once. Remember, adult supervision is essential at this age, for safety as well as peace.

container. Lauren looks up; their eyes meet. Carefully, deliberately, she puts down her shovel, picks up her container, and holds it out to Aaron. He digs again, pours the sand into the offered pail. They grin at each other delightedly. They have invented a game.

"In some ways Piaget and other early child development specialists underestimated children's abilities," comments Martin. "In particular, they didn't pay much attention to the interaction between children and their parents or caregivers." There is a real difference, Martin notes, in the way toddlers play with their peer group and how they play with family members and other "intimates." With these experienced and trusted guides, toddlers get their first taste of more complex co-operative play:

Aaron has just been introduced to ring-around-a-rosy. "Hands, hands," he begs, holding my hand to start another round. When his brothers enter the room, he immediately runs over to them, takes their hands, and pulls them into the game. We all fall down over and over, me surreptitiously choreographing the landing trajectories so everyone's head remains intact.

While these more structured games are fun and valuable, they generally cast a toddler in the role of "follower." In solitary play, a toddler can follow her own star, without the constraints of someone else's rules or expectations. And in parallel play with a comfortable companion, she can sometimes have the best of both worlds—open-ended play that she controls, along with the pleasure and learning that come from even our earliest social relationships.

People, Big and Small:
Becoming Social

Pete Gaffney

OF COURSE, YOUR TODDLER IS already passionately attached to *you*. But now, as she discovers the world beyond the family, she's figuring out how to relate to new people: her relatives, her caregiver, the children at playgroup.

Other children, especially, are so enticing—but how can she communicate and get along with a new friend, especially if neither of them can even talk much yet? Toddlers can really enjoy being together, but their encounters tend to be punctuated with tears and conflict. It's not fair to see this as being "aggressive" or "mean." It's more like what happens when two clumsy people make their first attempt at dancing together.

Toddlers will go through stages when they are more or less socially adventurous. One day she'll be chirping "Hi!" to everyone she passes in the mall, delighted when she gets a reply and crushed when she doesn't. A month later she may be in a more cautious phase, and hide her face when a well-meaning neighbour asks her a question.

Through her social ups and downs, though, you may already be able to get an overall sense of your child's social style. Some toddlers will bustle right into any group of kids and greet a new visitor with an enthusiastic hug. Others are reserved: they're intimidated by a crowded water-play table and save their chatter and hugs for people they know well. Don't worry; both introverts and extroverts can have satisfying, close relationships with others. Let your toddler relate to people in a way that's comfortable for her, and her social skills will grow.

"COOKAH, PEESE!": LEARNING TO TALK

WALKING, WITH ITS BUILT-IN DANGERS, may be more dramatic, but is anything more awe-inspiring than a toddler's mastery of speech? After long months of pointing or shrieking for what he wants, suddenly little Joe calmly requests a "cookah." How could you refuse? *And how did he do it?*

Gordon Wells, a professor at the Ontario Institute for Studies in Education who has extensively researched children's language acquisition, confirms that nothing we undertake in later life remotely compares with the enormous task of learning to talk. But that "cookah" didn't come out of nowhere. Joe's new words, and later phrases and sentences, grew out of language experiences he's explored since infancy.

Did you feel a bit silly, chatting away to your four-month-old as you changed her diaper? No need—it's that rich "language soup" heard by a baby that orients her to the sounds, rhythms and cadences of your mother tongue. (They don't call it that for nothing!) And every time you responded to her "rudimentary signs" (reaching, crying, smiling), says Wells, you were teaching her about how people communicate.

Most babies will say a "real" word within a few months of their first birthday. But in this, as in all things, every child is different. Between one and two, what your child can say isn't nearly as important as what he *understands*. Says Wells, "It is not all that uncommon for two-year-olds to produce only a few simple words. If they appear to understand what is said to them I wouldn't be too worried at this age."

As parents, we don't have to "teach" our children to talk. And we certainly shouldn't try to speed up their own developmental timetable by pushing them to speak early. But there is lots we can do to make learning to talk a happy and rewarding adventure.

Let's remember that communicating, not vocabulary lists, is what speech is all about. Wells suggests that the most important encourage-

---

THE OLDER SIBLING AS LANGUAGE COACH

My second child's first four-syllable word was: *ectoplasm*. How on earth would a two-year-old even be exposed to a word like that? A six-year-old brother and a cartoon called *Ghostbusters* on TV, that's how. A second or third child's early vocabulary is likely to be...well, a little different.

When it comes to language, older siblings are both inspired interpreters and relentless drill-masters. Dr. T. Berry Brazelton notes in *Toddlers and Parents* that siblings "correct, teach, and make the child repeat words and phrases after them until they are perfect...which places them under real pressure." Keep a casual eye on these interactions; big brother or sister may need a friendly reminder that too many corrections are discouraging, and that babies need to learn things at their own speed.

On the other hand, few adults could match the exuberance of language play between children. One mom recalls her two boys saying "armpit!" in funny voices over and over, laughing almost hysterically. For a toddler, this chance to experience language as sheer fun is priceless—don't be shy about joining in.

---

ment parents can offer is to make the child's efforts to communicate successful by showing you understand. His guidelines:

Assume what the child has to say is important and behave accordingly. (How would you feel if you tried to order a meal in a foreign language and the waiter just shrugged and turned away?)

Babies' first words are often unclear, so **make sure that you understand the intended meaning before acting.** (In other words, confirm that Joe's "cookah" means cookie, not the cuckoo clock, before handing him a Teddy Graham.)

When you reply, **first acknowledge that you received her message.** (Some toddlers demand this confirming repetition anyway. If you don't say, "Yes! That's a doggy!" before adding "Isn't he cute?" they'll doggedly go on saying "doggy" until you do.)

Repeating a child's message is also a natural and tactful way of helping her learn. Rather than correcting her, simply let her hear how *you* say and use the word. Her natural mimicry will lead her to gradually refine her speech.

Many parents wonder whether they should talk "baby talk" to their little ones. Experts seem to agree that it makes sense to simplify your speech *somewhat* to help your baby understand. As Wells puts it, "Don't talk way over a child's head. But if you never go beyond what the child is actually capable of saying, he won't have a model to learn from." Remember that kids understand far more than they can say, and learn from your inflection and body language as well as your words. Talk naturally about the child's "here and now" (the sand on her hands or the stew you're making, not your plans for next week), and her own passionate interest will fuel her understanding.

On the other hand, many babies will invent their own "baby talk" words. Parents naturally enjoy these delightful variations on our language. And if a favourite few become entrenched in the whole family's vocabulary for a while (as in "Please pass the peeta budda"), it won't do a bit of harm.

Now is the time to feed your child's delight in the sounds of language.

IF YOU SUSPECT A PROBLEM
An undiagnosed hearing problem can lead to serious language delays. Ask your doctor to have your one-year-old's hearing checked if she isn't:

- **Babbling**
- **Showing interest in the sounds around her (airplanes, birds, music)**
- **Responding to your simple questions or directions**

Between two and three, speech skills blossom. If your child's language development concerns you, again start with your paediatrician or family physician. Young children with significant speech delays may be referred to a speech-language pathologist for assessment.

He may be suddenly very responsive to music and surprise you by earnestly singing along to a favourite tune. He may love for you to sing a favourite nursery song and let him fill in the rhymes. Simple stories with recurring phrases or funny sound effects invite gleeful participation. He doesn't need to understand all the words to enjoy hearing them. Picture books invite him to talk about what he sees with you.

One word may become a glorious obsession, as your child matches up the concept with its verbal symbol; "cars" will be triumphantly pointed out on the street, in magazines, in toy stores. And your baby's sense of humour will bloom along with his speech; one toddler's favourite joke was to insist her father was a dog. ("Daddy. Do-do. Arf-arf!")

A child beginning to talk is taking a courageous leap into the world of human communication, inviting us to share her meanings. And when it comes right down to it, all we really have to do is to joyfully accept the invitation. It's that easy—and that important.

TOO CLOSE FOR COMFORT: THE SHY TODDLER

TWO-YEAR-OLD LISA HIDES BEHIND the furniture every time her grandparents come by to visit. If she's out shopping with her mother and a stranger speaks to her, even in a friendly and gentle tone of voice, she bursts into tears. When her mother took her to storytime at the library, Lisa wouldn't even look at the woman reading the book out loud. Her mother says, "I guess she's shy."

While Lisa is shy now, she may not always be. Most parents of a toddler have experienced occasional bouts of shyness (sometimes called "making strange"), when their child buries his face in a parental shoulder and refuses to even look at Aunt Nettie. Many quickly get over this initial reaction and become the life of the party. With other children, shyness seems to be a more basic part of their personality, and they continue to be uneasy in the presence of unfamiliar and sometimes even familiar faces.

Lenore Perkins's daughter Catherine was, according to her mother, "shy from birth." Lenore says, "She needed to be in physical contact with me all the time in order to feel safe around other people. If we went to a friend's home I never had to worry that Catherine might damage something, because she always stayed on my lap or right beside me."

If someone spoke directly to Catherine, she'd sometimes cry, especially if the speaker was male or had a loud voice. And even around adults she knew fairly well, Catherine was reluctant to speak up for herself. Instead, she'd whisper to her brother or another child and ask him to pass on the message.

Sometimes Catherine's shyness just overwhelmed her. She adored her exuberant and noisy uncles, for example, and eagerly looked forward to their visits. But when they walked in the front door, she'd run upstairs and hide in her room.

Lenore adds, "If you had seen her face, you'd know she couldn't help it. Sometimes when I held her I could hear her little heart pounding, and I knew she was just frightened by the situation. I think parents should know, too, that this isn't caused by overprotectiveness or something the parents have done wrong. It's just a personality trait some children have."

When Nicholas Beattie was two, he appeared to be shy with other children. "We'd go to a local drop-in play program or the park," recalls his mother, Renée. "And he would avoid any children he didn't know. He wouldn't go on a climber if other kids were on it, and he would stand so far back in line for the slide that other children would run ahead if I didn't help him keep his place." This trait continued into nursery school, where Nicholas did make a couple of friends but "would never just 'join in' with a group of kids at the water table or block centre. He'd wait until it was free for just him and his friend."

By elementary school, though, Nicholas was part of a large and noisy group of friends. "You would never describe him as 'shy' now," remarks Renée. "In fact, he tends to be a little too goofy in class and appears to be quite extroverted."

Whether a toddler's shyness is an inborn personality trait or a passing phase, parents can help best by respecting their child's feelings and helping her to feel more comfortable, not by pushing. Wendy Asher, manager of child-care services at St. Clair College in Windsor, Ontario, explains, "Forcing the issue never works—it just makes a shy child withdraw further. What they need is lots of acceptance and encouragement, but no pressure."

Lenore realized that punishing Catherine or trying to force her into social situations would only make things worse. Since Catherine was calm as long as her mother was with her, Lenore continued taking her on visits to friends, relatives and community events, but allowed her daughter to sit on her lap or stay close by. She asked her friends and rel-

INTRODUCING AUNT NETTIE

While some children *are* temperamentally shy, Penelope Leach feels that most "stranger anxiety" in toddlers has more to do with how adults commonly approach young children. "We don't rush up to adult strangers, or even our neighbours, and kiss them or put them on our laps," she points out. "And we'd be jolly anxious if anyone tried that with us!" Getting to know someone, she observes, takes time and sensitivity. All too often, babies are pushed into an intimacy they're not ready for. Instead, Leach suggests we:

- Hang back and let the baby make the first move. If you don't scare him off, a toddler's own curiosity and sociability will eventually prevail.
- Remain aware of the baby. Some potential friendships never get off the ground because the adult, engrossed in grown-up talk, misses a toddler's first tentative overtures.
- Don't assume she remembers you. "You need to be around pretty frequently before you qualify as a 'familiar person' at this age," Leach advises. "A grandparent, for example, who sees the baby once a month may have to sit back and wait for the child's approach all over again at each visit." Later, as your child is able to recognize her grandparents in a photo album, and keep their memory alive by talking about them, there will be more continuity to their relationship.

atives to give Catherine a little time to warm up before they tried to speak to her, pick her up or involve her in activities.

At the childcare centre, Asher and her staff work with parents in helping their shy children adjust. She finds that consistency is very important—the child needs to know what is going to happen and which staff member she will be with. Often they try to match a more outgoing child, who is familiar with the centre, with a new, shy child to "show them the ropes."

Most important, Asher believes, is an attitude of acceptance. "It's

THE TODDLER-FRIENDLY VISITOR: A CASE STUDY

My first two boys were "slow to warm up" with new people at this age. Or rather, most new people. One out-of-town friend, Kate, visited infrequently but never failed to win over our "toddler of the year." Here's a typical scenario that shows how Kate managed to invite without overwhelming:

Kate arrives at the door. We hug, hang up her coat, settle her into the living room—all with 18-month-old Jesse stuck on my hip. Kate makes a point of saying hi to Jesse by name, but doesn't go any further. We talk for a while, and Jesse eventually wiggles off my lap and cruises around. He feigns disinterest, but he's checking out Kate as he plays. Soon he sidles up to her with a ball. She notices. "What've you got there, Jesse?"

"Baw." He plops it in her lap and scurries off. Soon he's back with a stuffed bear. "Bear" joins "baw" on Kate's lap. On the third trip back, Kate's ready with her hand outstretched. "Thanks. Want to show me your book?" She slips down on the floor and opens the pages. Soon Jesse is snuggled up beside her, pointing out his favourite jungle animals. It's love at—well, second sight.

okay for shy children to sit on the side and watch if they want; they don't have to jump in and take part. Shy children tend to remain shy, but they gradually become more comfortable—in their own quiet way."

Catherine, at seven, agrees. "I'm still shy," she says. But she seems confident and comfortable in most situations, and that, says Asher, is exactly what parents of shy children should aim for.

LITTLE ROUGHNECKS: TAMING AGGRESSIVE BEHAVIOUR

OU'VE TRIED TO BE A LOVING, nurturing parent since the day little Jasmine was born. Then one day your sweet, adorable toddler barrels into your neighbour's little boy and bites him on the arm. A week later you catch her punching her cousin because he was playing with a toy she wanted. What happened to that nonviolent child you were raising?

"If you ask parents to describe their toddler's behaviours, many of them express concerns about aggressive behaviours, and most of them are surprised by them—they never thought their children would do these things," says Dr. Elizabeth Levin, professor of psychology at Laurentian University in Sudbury, Ontario. "But, in fact, these behaviours are normal and common."

Toddlers by nature are very physical creatures. They don't have the verbal skills to express their feelings of frustration and anger, so those feelings tend to come out physically. Jasmine might throw a toy on the floor when she can't figure out how to make it work. When another child isn't doing what she wants she also may lash out and whack him.

Children in this age group don't have a real sense of how their actions affect others. When we point out that little Johnny is now crying because he was hit with the toy truck, a young toddler isn't able to understand how the other child feels. It will take many simple explanations ("That hurts Johnny!"), and more life experience, before the truth that is so obvious to us—that when you hit someone, they feel the way you would if you were hit—is obvious to him.

Levin also points out that it's the toddlers who are most interested in interacting with other children who tend to be the most aggressive. But this apparent "aggression" is not malicious. Like overenthusiastic puppies, these kids have a tendency to come on a little strong. As they learn

IS IT MORE THAN A STAGE?

When is a toddler's aggressive behaviour more than just a stage? When should parents be concerned?

Psychology professor Elizabeth Levin suggests considering the fighting in the context of the child's whole life:

- Does it happen primarily with one particular friend or at a certain time (such as when she is tired or hungry)?
- Has it started just after some changes in the family, such as the arrival of a new baby?
- Does the child seem otherwise cheerful and happy?

If so, the aggressive behaviour is probably not a serious concern.

However, if you notice that your child is hitting many people, in a wide variety of situations, and that his attacks seem to be getting more frequent, then it would be worth investigating. "It may be that this child simply has a slower-developing sense of self-control," Levin says, "but it's worth exploring with a professional."

more about the give-and-take of relationships with others, and develop their verbal skills, their "little roughneck" approach to friendships will subside.

But how do you deal with it? Should you just sit by while Jacob pounds on Alyssa's back to get her toys away from her, waiting for him to grow out of it?

"While this behaviour is normal, parents shouldn't be particularly tolerant of it," Levin advises. "It's also important not to respond aggressively yourself, because then you're modelling that behaviour. Try removing the child from the setting or redirecting the activity. Show your disapproval in a calm, friendly way."

Vigilance is essential. If you know your toddler is likely to bite or hit another child, stay close by and watch her, so that you can intervene *before* she connects. Pay attention, too, to the kinds of situations that get her overexcited. She may relate better to other children in a park than in a crowded play room, in a one-on-one situation, or if free play is interspersed with quiet, adult-mediated activities like reading stories or drawing with sidewalk chalk. Every successful experience in getting along with others, and every example she sees of "gentle" play, will help. So will time.

Aggressive behaviour in very young children does not mean they will continue to be aggressive when they get older (although, of course, some will). When two-year-old Justin started acting bossy and aggressive with his younger playmate, Miles, it put a crimp into their mothers' weekly get-together. "It was a real strain," admits Miles's mother. "Justin started grabbing and pushing, and Miles eventually acted the perfect victim by bursting into tears the moment Justin even looked like he *might* do something. How do you handle that? You want to protect your child. You're embarrassed for your friend. Luckily, neither of us over-reacted. But for a few months we rarely got to talk in peace—we were too busy mediating."

"When our puppy was biting, we were told to give him lots of exercise and lots of chew toys, to avoid aggressive games that got him overexcited, and to stop playing immediately whenever he nipped. I think we handled our toddler in more or less the same way!"

While some parents might have decided to look for a more closely matched playmate for their child, these mothers hung in. "We just spent more time playing *with* the kids for a while, and I tried to make sure that Justin didn't have the opportunity to harass Miles," recalls Justin's mother, Alida. "We intended to be friends for a long time, so it was worth riding out a little conflict."

Their patience and close supervision paid off. As Justin and Miles both became more verbal, the "bullying" stopped. Justin was never aggressive with any other children. The two boys are now 11 years old, and the best of friends.

Once parents understand that aggression is common in toddlers and

BITING

While few aggressive actions dismay parents more than biting, from a baby's point of view it's no different from hitting or pushing. Frustration and overstimulation tend to trigger biting in some children, so preventive planning can help. "Simplify the situation," advises parent educator Kathy Lynn. "Fewer children, shorter play periods, frequent 'quiet time' breaks with a parent, less demand for sharing toys—all of these will lower the frustration quotient, and incidentally allow the adults to monitor the situation more closely." If your child has a biting habit, stay near when he's playing with other children, so you can move right in and scoop him up as soon as you see a potential bite in the making.

And please, says Lynn, *don't* bite her back. "It really doesn't make sense, because it's modelling the behaviour you want to discourage," she says. "But even if it worked, it's a horrible thing to do!"

Most toddler bites cause no lasting harm. But if a bite actually breaks the skin, there is a high risk of infection. Wash the wound well with soap and water, and seek medical attention. The physician will want to be sure the child's tetanus immunization is up to date, and will want any signs of developing infection reported right away.

rarely a cause for concern, they are able to deal with the problem without getting angry, Levin finds. That's important—children need a calm parent to steer them back onto the road of developing self-control and handling their frustrations with words instead of actions.

"MINE!": THE POSSESSIVE TODDLER

"N o-no, Ry-Ry, my truck!" Twenty-month-old Jeremy barrelled across the room and rescued his precious truck from his playgroup friend—the same truck he had been "sharing" unconcernedly for the past six months. The next fifteen minutes of their visit were uproarious, as Jeremy frantically attempted to salvage every toy Riley touched, to the inevitable wails of protest. Finally, a snack and a batch of playdough saved the day, and as Jeremy became more involved in play, he forgot about guarding his toys. His mom eventually got over her embarrassment, too—especially once other children in the playgroup starting showing the same behaviour with *their* toys.

Kimberley Tremblay can relate. "When we first saw Megan act that way, we thought maybe we had a greedy little tyrant on our hands. Now we know that she's normal." Tremblay remembers when her own playgroup was a peaceful get-together of babies involved in parallel play. "Now they're learning to play *with* each other, and there's a lot more fighting and tussles over toys. But we all realize that it's not a negative reflection on the kids or parents, it's just part of behaviour at that age."

But why is it? What's so difficult, after all, about allowing another child to have a turn with your toy, your chair, or even your dad? Barbara Morrongiello, a developmental psychologist at the University of Guelph, explains why possessiveness and toddlerhood often go hand in hand: "This comes from their stage of cognitive development, how they understand the world, the limited way that they can think."

Unlike a younger baby, toddlers are developing a sense of their own separate selfhood. They're beginning to grasp the concept of possession—specifically, of their own possessions (although to most toddlers, "mine" seems to mean something closer to "I have it" or "I want it"). However, "They think 'now,' versus an adult who can think in the

129

LEARNING TO SHARE

Even though it may be a long time before your toddler can share with any kind of consistency, you can start to lay the groundwork now:

- "We try to model sharing ourselves," says Kimberley Tremblay. "Little kids don't even know what you mean by 'share.' So I'll say, 'I'm going to share my chips with Daddy' or 'Would you like to share my cookie?' and act really appreciative when she shares something with me."

- "We also talk about feelings. Megan is learning the different names for feelings, and I'll point out how other kids are feeling—'Adam is sad. He wanted to try out the slide.'"

- Childcare professional Alice Davidson suggests that young children can start to get familiar with ideas like taking turns and sharing through simple, nonthreatening play with their parents. Taking turns choosing something funny to put on during dress-up play or making animal noises, or passing a plate of crackers back and forth (casually using the words 'my turn' and 'your turn') are all experiences that may lay the groundwork for her eventual social graces.

future," says Morrongiello. "And their thinking is 'egocentric' or self-centred, which has a negative tone but just means that they really are not capable of thinking about how another person feels." So young Jeremy was not yet able to take himself through a thinking process that adults take for granted: "I will get my truck back again later. The truck is still mine even though my friend is using it. If I take it away he will be upset."

"I think you have to be patient, and realize that sharing is a skill that takes time to learn," says Cynthia Hooper, mother of a just-two-year-old (Elizabeth) and an eight-month-old baby (Emily). Elizabeth can be quite possessive with her sister, grabbing toys from her and insisting on the first hug when Hooper picks them up from daycare. Hooper protects Elizabeth's right to some of her own possessions—notably her Barney and "Baby Sue"—but she's also gently working on helping her daughter develop better tactics. "I say things like 'It's more fun for Emily if she has a toy, too,' and encourage her to either give back the toy or find another that Emily will like. I encourage her to put her special things up where the baby can't get them, and I've been trying to teach her how to distract the baby with something else when Emily's heading for her stuff."

Alice Davidson is the drop-in co-ordinator at the Parent Resource Centre in Ottawa, and she sees toddlers clutching toys every single day. "It bothers parents a lot," she acknowledges, "but a toddler who says 'mine!' is not being selfish, he's being self-centred, and that's healthy. You want him to be self-centred at two."

Playdates go more smoothly at this age, suggests Davidson, with some advance planning. "Set up a strategy that respects your child's need to be possessive," says Davidson. "Before visitors come, tell your child, 'Someone is coming to visit. If there are special things you don't want anyone to play with, we can put those things away.' And try to arrange to have doubles of popular toys—two riding toys, two little chairs—perhaps by asking the friend to bring along some extras."

"My son used to like to play 'Santa Claus': I would pretend to sleep while he snuck in with a bagful of little toys. Then I would wake up, admire my presents, thank him profusely, and give them right back. It gave him the satisfaction of sharing, without the anxiety."

Because toddlers don't really understand "the future," taking turns is another concept that takes a while to understand. "I definitely think that when another child has her toy, Megan doesn't realize that she will get it back," muses Tremblay. While most toddlers are not yet able to plan ahead and organize a strategy like taking turns, the parents at Tremblay's playgroup have developed a routine that seems to work well. "There are usually three or four kids in the group, and sometimes they all want the same toy. So the routine is, we set the timer and everyone gets a 30-second turn. (We tried one minute at first, but that was too long for them to wait!) They know now what to expect, and usually it works pretty well."

While we can't rush a child's "inner developmental timetable," we can gently introduce the values and concepts that will help him learn to share when he's ready. Morrongiello says, "Cognitive development unfolds to some extent independent of our input. But we do also teach nurturing, empathy, and responsibility for behaviour. It's a long-term process. Sometimes when I'm explaining something to my three-year-old I realize, 'This time he understood a bit more. The pieces are filling in, unfolding.'"

It's understandable that in their first encounters with ownership and control, little ones may go a little overboard at first. And it's important to respect the strong feelings they may have about their possessions. As Morrongiello points out, "We all have special things that we don't want to share, and it's not unreasonable to feel that way."

"Sometimes," concludes Davidson, "you have to stand up for your child and say, 'He isn't ready to share yet.'"

"I KISS IT BETTER": TODDLERS CAN BE KIND

I HAS BECOME A TRUISM TO ASSERT that toddlers are *egocentric*. They can't be expected to share, be fair, or think of other's feelings, because they cannot yet see the world through another's eyes. *Their* wishes, *their* goals, *their* needs and feelings, are all they are really aware of. Empathy? Consideration? Out of their league.

Inasmuch as it helps us parents to have realistic expectations of our children, this insight is very valuable. For example, when we find ourselves thinking irritably, "Can't she see that I need some time alone?" we can remind ourselves that no, she really can't. Little people are not, as a rule, able to look after other people's needs.

And yet...

Katie delights in giving her mother bites of her snacks.

Carey runs over to the carriage when the baby starts to cry. He pulls up her blanket, pats her back, and croons, "There, there, it okay."

Tara jumps up and accidentally bumps her dad's chin. She carefully kisses the sore spot, asking, "All better?"

Jason jealously guards his toys, wresting away anything his friend, David, touches. But when David finally starts to cry, Jason stops in his tracks. After a few moments of worried observation, he runs up to David and thrusts the toy he had wanted into his lap.

Is this just imitative behaviour? Or is it something more?

"It really is important not to expect too much from toddlers," cautions Professor Janet Sayer, a developmental psychologist at Simon Fraser University who has studied the development of empathy in children. "Yet we certainly see the beginnings of both empathy and kindness in children this young."

Strayer points out that empathy—sharing another's emotions—is often what motivates us to act kindly towards that person. But empathy

MORE TIPS ON TEACHING KINDNESS

Michael Schulman and Eva Mekler, authors of *Bringing Up a Moral Child* (Doubleday, 1994), have a few more simple suggestions for starting toddlers on the road to kind behaviour:

- **Make him feel loved. This, say the authors, is the cornerstone for children's moral development, the "base" from which they learn how to love and care for others.**
- **Teach the word "gentle" or "nice." When your child roughly explores another child, a pet, or your face, say, "Be gentle," then take her hand and stroke softly with it, repeating the word. Stroke her softly, too, again saying "nice" or "gentle."**
- **Teach "ouch." Use the word "ouch" when she hurts herself. Later, if she hurts someone else, saying "ouch" will help her understand how that person feels.**
- **Play give-and-take. Young toddlers love "giving" you things. Be appreciative, smile, and say thank-you. Act equally happy to give it back to him. It feels good to give.**

can also be an uncomfortable or overwhelming sensation, especially for a toddler who hasn't quite differentiated between another's distress and his own. Understanding that can help us to understand a toddler's sometimes disturbing responses to another's pain:

Alyssa is crying after bumping her elbow at daycare. Her little friend, Erik, finds her special "blanky," and brings it to her. He gets a warm word of appreciation from his teacher. But Jessica takes one look at Alyssa, and bursts into tears herself. Karin retreats to the far end of the room, determinedly turning her back on the whole scene. And Zack become so agitated that he runs up to Alyssa, scowling, and yells "Stop it!"

In this example, says Strayer, Erik has been able to empathize with

Alyssa, and even to think of a kind act to help her. Jessica picks up Alyssa's emotions, but they trigger her own upset feelings—something Strayer terms "emotional contagion." Karin and Zack respond, says Strayer, with a kind of "empathy gone off track"—they are emotionally aroused by Alyssa's distress, so unpleasantly that they focus on relieving their *own* anxiety—either by avoiding the whole scene, or in Zack's case, by attacking what he sees as its source.

What we may not realize is that Jessica, Karin and Zack all need comforting and reassurance, too.

"Not long after my second baby was born, I was sick with the flu and feeling very sorry for myself, with these two little kids to care for—until Lily, my toddler, came over and solemnly pulled up her shirt and offered to breastfeed me, 'so you feel better.' I guess she could see that it usually worked with the baby . . ."

"They need to be told and shown that they're safe while feeling this," suggests Strayer, "and helped to see that although Alyssa is hurt, they are not."

What else can parents and caregivers do to help toddler learn about empathy?

Strayer has a few simple suggestions:

The golden rule. Toddlers are great imitators, so if we model kindness, they will try out that behaviour. And Strayer observes that (like all of us, but more obviously) toddlers are only able to care about and reach out to others when they feel safe and secure themselves. (That's why your toddler can share happily when it's *her choice*, but not when she's feeling pressured or threatened.) When Mom and Dad can be counted on for emotional support, that's a big security boost!

Observe and talk about feelings—his own and other people's. With a toddler, this needs to be kept very simple: "Grandpa will be so happy to see you." "Did that clown make you feel scared?" "We're having fun at this party, but Anna is feeling shy. She needs to sit with her mom right now." You are introducing two pretty sophisticated concepts: that feelings can be named, even though you can't see them; and that other people might not feel the same things that you do.

Allow your child to experience an appropriate range of emotions. Obviously, we're not talking about overwhelming children with horror movies, screaming battles, or heartrending stories. We want to encourage empathy, not nightmares! But Strayer points out, "If we artificially protect our children from emotional discomforts, they may have a harder time understanding people's feelings."

When your child is sad or angry, think about helping him to deal with those feelings, rather than trying to "turn them off." Respect your child's sensitivity level, but don't automatically censor the sad parts of stories—children are no strangers to sadness, and knowing that others share these feelings can even be reassuring.

Above all, show your appreciation and approval when your toddler acts with kindness—even if it doesn't work out so well. When Aunt Florence bumps her head on the cupboard door, she may be taken aback by little Hailey's offer of her pacifier, and a clumsy hug may be the last thing your colicky baby needs. But the generous spirit that prompted these "gifts"—now that's something *everybody* needs.

Last Words:
A Fond Farewell to Toddlerhood

Erin Prendergast

TWO-YEAR-OLDS GET A LOT OF BAD PRESS. In fact, the "Terrible Twos" have acquired legendary status as the most dreaded childhood stage, second only to the all-too-similar Awful Adolescence. Even Penelope Leach, that most sympathetic childhood champion, describes the two-year-old's transition into pre-schoolerhood in distinctly unflattering terms: "...he ceases to be a wayward, confusing, unpredictable and often balky person-in-the-making, and becomes a comparatively co-operative, eager-and-easy-to-please real human being..."

Don't believe everything you read. Kids don't sprout fangs and horns on their second birthday. In fact, lots of us treasure the so-called Terrible Twos as our favourite age. What's so terrific about Twos?

They talk. "I love the freedom that language brings," says Sheila Collett, mother of two-year-old Heather. "We can talk about what's going to happen. She can negotiate instead of going to pieces. And I can figure out what's bothering her." On a recent camping trip, Heather was inexplicably distressed at the sight of air mattresses at the beach (they were sleeping on air mattresses in their tent). Only when Heather finally blurted out, "*My* mattress won't go in the water!" were Sheila and her husband, Ben, able to reassure Heather that no, she wasn't going to wake up afloat.

Sheila also enjoys how language reveals "the blossoming of her imagination, and her sense of humour." My own little boy, nodding with mock seriousness at being told not to touch broken glass, intoned, "Yeah. That's right. It might get into Grandma's house and mix up in her food." A neighbour's son, talking up his approaching bedtime ritual with a salesman's enthusiasm, concluded, "It'll be beautiful, Dad!" Two-year-olds really do say the darnedest things.

Once children start to talk, we glimpse how they think and learn. "Dat where we did go!" she crows excitedly, looking at last year's pictures of the cottage. Would you ever have guessed she'd remember that long ago?

They are learning at a breathtaking pace. It's a marvel how a two-year-old takes on Life. "All of a sudden they have amazing abilities," says Sue Fortin. "It's frightening, sometimes, what they can get into. But you have to admire the determination and persistence that get them there." An adult with the learning skills of a two-year-old would be formidable, indeed.

They have the cuddliest little bodies. By next year, she'll be a long, leggy preschooler. Nothing wrong with that. But this is your last chance for "baby" cuddles: the last time she'll be compact enough to carry her a long way, to swoop her upside-down and boop her belly 15 times just to hear that delicious laugh, to curl her up in a little ball on your lap and rock her. You can do all these things with older kids, but it's definitely more awkward.

Nobody in the world is as unselfconsciously appealing. A two-year-old in a sunny mood can charm the pants off anybody. Watch him dancing or singing along to music, playing a chasing game, whispering to his bear, kissing your sore finger, chatting up Grandma. Can you help smiling?

"At this age even their self-assertion is cute," says Sue. At a recent school book fair, passers-by grinned at the toddler who stomped his foot at his dad and defiantly retorted, "It's *not* time to go! Now I mean it!" Even the father, hearing his own phrase flung back at him, had to laugh.

They love you uncritically. Unless coached by an older sibling, a two-year-old is unlikely to tell you your breath smells bad, your clothes aren't cool, or your rules are dumb. She'll get really, really mad at you, but she's basically blind to your faults. This is definitely to be enjoyed while it lasts.

There's a poignancy about a two-year-old that springs from the way she embodies both baby and child. She's become aware of her own will and abilities (although her reach often exceeds her grasp). But she hasn't given up the dependency of babyhood and needs to be reassured of your protection and love. Of course that's where the conflicts and frustrations of the age stem from, too. She'll beg to go to a friend's house and then spend the visit glued around your neck; cower with fear at a fly but try to pat the lion at the zoo.

Celebrate your Two's efforts to grow up. Help him find safe, appropriate ways to exert his independence. But cherish the baby along with the emerging child. You'll miss him when he's gone.